THE STORY OF OUR COLLEGES
1835–1935

THE TUTORS OF THE SEVEN COLLEGES AT THE TIME OF METHODIST UNION.

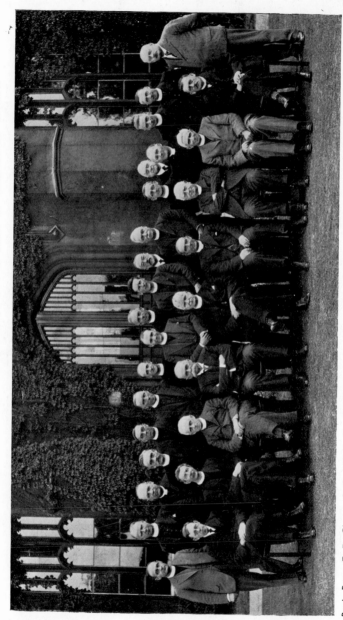

Back Row—F. B. Clogg, C. R. North, Dr. H. Bett, Dr. C. Ryder Smith, W. B. Brash, Dr. E. S. Waterhouse, Dr. L. F. Church, Dr. H. Watkin-Jones, Dr. W. F. Howard, Dr. C. J. Wright, G. G. Hornby, A. L. Humphries, Dr. H. G. Meecham, E. W. Hirst, Dr. R. N. Flew, Dr. J. A. Findlay, Dr. V. Taylor, Atkinson Lee.

Front Row—J. T. Brewis, Dr. W. F. Lofthouse, T. H. Barratt, E. S. Lamplough, Dr. J. H. Ritson, T. Naylor, Dr. J. W. Lightley, Dr. H. M. Hughes, Dr. W. I. Wardle.

Frontispiece

THE STORY OF OUR COLLEGES

1835-1935

A CENTENARY RECORD
OF
MINISTERIAL TRAINING
IN THE
METHODIST CHURCH

BY

W. BARDSLEY BRASH
M.A., B.Lit., B.D.

LONDON
THE EPWORTH PRESS
(Edgar C. Barton)
25-35 CITY ROAD, E.C.1

Made and Printed in Great Britain by the KEMP HALL PRESS, LTD.
in the City of Oxford

CONTENTS

CHAP.   PAGE

PREFACE 7

I. JOHN WESLEY AND THE EARLY METHODIST PREACHERS 11

II. THE STRUGGLE FOR A THEOLOGICAL INSTITUTION 23

III. HOXTON THEOLOGICAL INSTITUTION . 34

IV. HOXTON AND ABNEY HOUSE . . . 42

V. DIDSBURY 55

VI. RICHMOND 69

VII. HEADINGLEY 79

VIII. HANDSWORTH 92

IX. RE-OPENING OF THREE COLLEGES—THE COMING OF WESLEY HOUSE, CAMBRIDGE 103

X. A GREAT CRUSADE 112

XI. HARTLEY PRIMITIVE METHODIST COLLEGE By A. L. Humphries, M.A.
    (1) The Story of the Building . . 123
    (2) The Inner Life of the College . 135

XII. VICTORIA PARK AND RANMOOR COLLEGES By G. G. Hornby, M.A., B.D.
    (1) Free Methodist College . . 148
    (2) Ranmoor College . . . 152
    (3) United Methodist College . . 157
    (4) The College after Union . . 160

EPILOGUE—AFTER UNION 164

ILLUSTRATIONS

TUTORS OF THE SEVEN COLLEGES AT THE
TIME OF METHODIST UNION . . *Frontispiece*

Facing page

A COLLEGE CHAPEL 32

DIDSBURY COLLEGE 64

RICHMOND COLLEGE 72

HEADINGLEY COLLEGE 80

HANDSWORTH COLLEGE 96

ENTRANCE TO WESLEY HOUSE, CAMBRIDGE . . 104

HARTLEY VICTORIA COLLEGE 128

VICTORIA PARK COLLEGE 160

PREFACE

We hope that the readers of this book will realize the difficulties with which we have had to contend. It is, of course, impossible to tell, in a short space, the story of the Methodist Theological Colleges (1835–1935). We realized this when we began our task. We have sought, however, to show the main trends of progress, to tell a few of the chief incidents in the story, and to picture some of the leading personalities. We have been compelled, by lack of room, to leave out many things which we should have liked to have mentioned, and to omit the names of many who have made great contributions to the life of our Colleges. We hope that the reader will forgive us our omissions. Many noble men who have done much to mould the history of our Colleges find no place in this story. That was unavoidable : but it does not mean that we are unmindful of their splendid service.

We have, with a few exceptions, refrained from trying to picture the living. It would have been a delightful task to have told their story, but we decided that it would be more fittingly done, in A.D. 2035, by the men who will then write the Bicentenary volume.

My task has been to tell the story of the Colleges of the Wesleyan Methodist Church. Rev. A. L. Humphries, M.A., writes of the Hartley Primitive Methodist College, and Rev. G. G. Hornby, M.A., B.D., of Victoria Park and Ranmoor Colleges of the United Methodist Church. I take this opportunity of thanking them both for their help so freely given.

W. Bardsley Brash.

All Saints' Day,
  1935.
Didsbury College, Manchester.

7

' Howbeit when He, the Spirit of truth, is come, He shall guide you into all the truth : for He shall not speak from Himself; but what things soever He shall hear, these shall He speak : and He shall declare unto you the things that are to come.'

St. John's Gospel, XVI, 13.

' Wisdom is more mobile than any motion ;
Yea, she pervadeth and penetrateth all things by reason of her pureness.
For she is a breath of the power of God,
And a clear effluence of the glory of the Almighty ;
Therefore can nothing defiled find entrance into her.
For she is an effulgence from everlasting light,
And an unspotted mirror of the working of God,
And an image of His goodness.
And she, being one, can do all things ;
And remaining in herself, reneweth all things :
And from generation to generation passing into holy souls
She maketh them friends of God and prophets.
For nothing doth God love save him that dwelleth with Wisdom.'

Book of Wisdom.

' Let us now praise famous men, and our fathers that begat us.
The Lord manifested in them great glory,
Even His mighty power from the beginning.
Such as did bear rule in their kingdoms,
And were men renowned for their power,
Giving counsel by their understanding,
Such as have brought tidings in prophecies ;
Leaders of the people by their counsels,
And by their understanding men of learning for the people ;
Wise were their words in their instruction :

* * * *

All these were honoured in their generations,
And were a glory in their days.'

Ecclesiasticus.

9

CHAPTER I

JOHN WESLEY AND THE EARLY METHODIST PREACHERS

At the first Conference, in 1744, the following question was asked, ' Can we have a seminary for labourers ? ' The answer was, ' If God spare us till another Conference '. At the second Conference, in 1745, the question was asked again, ' Can we have a seminary for labourers yet ? ' The reply was, ' Not till God give us a proper tutor '.

It was not until ninety years after—in December 1834—the work was not started until the beginning of 1835—that the first seminary was opened for the training of Wesleyan ministers. It would, however, be a great mistake to imagine that during that long period nothing was done to increase the knowledge of the travelling preachers. John Wesley was born in an age of Reason, and in more ways than one he was a child of that age. His ' Appeals to Men of Reason', his thirst for knowledge, and his intellectual curiosity, show us a man who brought to religion the service of his *mind*. He was certainly no obscurantist. The child was father to the man. For of the boy Wesley we read that, when asked if he would take some bread or fruit, he would say, ' I thank you ; I will think of it '. There is nothing irrational about him. His father, Samuel Wesley, said to his wife, ' I profess, Sweetheart, I think our Jack would not attend to the most pressing necessities of nature unless he could give a reason '. We see this emphasis on Reason in his Oxford days, in Georgia, and on his return from Georgia. We notice this same insistence in his conversation with Peter Böhler. Peter Böhler said to John Wesley—in those days just before the time of deliverance—May 24, 1738—' My brother, my brother, you must be purged of your philosophy '. But that never happened. Wesley never ceased to have the philosopher's turn of mind. Nevertheless, he learned something of vital importance from Böhler, and that was to put Reason in its right place. Reason became for him the ally of Faith—and not its master.

> Where reason fails with all her powers,
> There faith prevails and love adores.

Wesley regarded Faith as dominant, but always welcomed the service of Reason—he knew full well from his own experience that there were certain heights she could not scale, but he followed her light, until it grew dim. He was a man of Faith and Reason. He eagerly accepted all the helps to Faith, and yet to him Faith was ever the guiding star. It is necessary to realize this—if we wish to understand Wesley and his views on education.

He was a man of one book—and that book was to him the touchstone of all things. He has declared this in his memorable words :

> ' I want to know one thing—the way to heaven. God Himself has condescended to teach me the way. He hath written it down in a book. O give me that book. At any price, give me the book of God. I have it ; here is knowledge enough for me. Let me be *homo unius libri*. Here then I am, far from the busy ways of men. I sit down alone : only God is here. In His presence I read His book ; for this end, to find the way to heaven.'

But for the understanding of that book he used all the helps he could find—linguistic, expository, philosophical. He was an omnivorous reader, and browsed in many fields of literature. His reading was not only intensive, but also extensive. In his criticism of books we can feel the incisiveness of his mind, and see his logical and critical faculty at work. Wesley could never have said with

Francis of Assisi, ' throw away your breviary ' : or with Joachim di Fiore, ' He who is truly a monk thinks nothing to be his—only a harp '.

He was truly a man of one book—because he was a man of many books. But the One Book was the supreme guide. It received light and meaning from other books, but was the master-light of all his seeing. His quarrel with the Moravians arose because some of them denied the means of grace—refused to pray, to receive the Communion, and to read the Bible. This was anathema to him, because it was irrational. He would use all the means of grace. He would learn from any and every quarter. But we must realize that he never mistook the means for the end. It is in this sense that Wesley is a man of his Century—and is not. For he is a lover of Reason—but also an adorer of Grace. We have lingered on this subject because it is the key which unlocks the door which gives us entrance to many secret chambers in Wesley's life. He is first and foremost an evangelist. The work of the United Societies is to call men to God and to spread scriptural holiness throughout the land. To reach this goal, he needs men aflame with the love of God. That is the *sine qua non*. But he asks for men who, having the passion for souls, will use their minds, read the Bible, submit to training, and grasp every means possible to improve their knowledge. It was for this reason that, at his second Conference, he asked, ' Can we have a seminary for labourers yet ? ' The reply is characteristic of Wesley, for though it comes in the ' Minutes of some conversations between the Rev. Mr. Wesley and others ', the questions and answers were obviously his—' Not till God give us a proper tutor '.

When Wesley could not reach his goal one way, he found it by another. He had two desires for his preachers, one that they should devote themselves with fiery enthusiasm to the work of evangelism, and the other was that each travelling preacher should ' give diligence to present himself approved unto God, a workman who needeth not to be ashamed, handling aright the word of truth '. Wesley, we believe, asked of his followers two things—an entrance, by conversion, into the Kingdom of God, and a willingness to learn the ways and laws of that Kingdom. He called men to God, and then inspired and trained them to seek to know His will and way more fully. We see that this was his method at the opening of his great campaign, and he continued it throughout his long ministry. We will quote the entry in the *Journal*—for April 2, 1739—which tells of his first preaching in the open air : ' At four in the afternoon I submitted to be more vile, and proclaimed in the highways the glad tidings of salvation to about three thousand people. The Scripture on which I spoke was this—(is it possible that any one should be ignorant that it is fulfilled in every true minister of Christ ?)—" The Spirit of the Lord is upon me because he hath anointed me to preach the Gospel to the poor. He hath sent me to heal the broken-hearted ; to preach deliverance to the captives, and recovery of sight to the blind : to set at liberty them that are bruised, to proclaim the acceptable year of the Lord ".' Let us note carefully what follows—' At seven I began expounding " The Acts of the Apostles " to a Society Meeting in Baldwin Street '. That was Wesley's way—it was wisely two-fold—evangelistic and educative.

Alexander Knox—who knew Wesley well, and never lost his love for him, although he parted from him ecclesiastically, and is hailed to-day by many as one of the earliest prophets of the Oxford Movement—said that John Wesley was an excellent foundation and super-structure man. By this somewhat clumsy phrase he meant that Wesley called men to God, and then taught them the meaning and the implications of their faith. Now if this be so, it is evident that he would demand in his preachers this two-fold quality. He asked for preachers aflame with evangelical fire, and able and ready to give a reason for the hope that was in them. He desired men who could lay the foundation, and raise the superstructure. It is of immense importance to grasp this fact. It accounts for the emphasis of Methodism on its work of training men for the ministry. Its ministers were from the beginning men whose hearts God had touched, who were primarily preachers of the Gospel. They were the heralds of the Kingdom, as truly as the followers of St. Francis, who joyously boasted that his friars were the heralds of the King. Wesley realized that one loving heart sets another loving heart on fire —but he never made this a cover for ignorance. He knew that, besides a knowledge that puffeth up, there is a knowledge which edifieth, and he sought in every way possible to make the itinerating preachers men learned in the Scriptures, and to train their minds.

We learn from John Wesley's *Journal* that he often gathered his preachers together to inform their minds, as well as to kindle their hearts. Under the date, March 4, 1747, we read : ' This week I read over with some young men a Compendium of Rhetoric and a System of Ethics. I see not why a man of tolerable understanding may not learn in six months' time more of solid philosophy than is commonly learned at Oxford in four (perhaps seven) years '. In March 1749, he goes to Kingswood School, which, owing its inception to George Whitefield, had been a school for the children of the Kingswood colliers ; then while in its early and small beginnings was taken over by John Wesley, and became also a school for the sons of travelling preachers, and at times a training ground for his preachers. He writes in his *Journal* : ' My design was to have as many of our preachers here (at Kingswood) during the Lent as could be spared : and to read lectures to them every day, as I did to my pupils in Oxford. I had seventeen of them in all. These I divided into two classes, and read to one Bishop Pearson *On the Creed*, to the other Aldrich's *Logic* and to both

Rules of Action and Utterance'. It is interesting to note that Wesley, when storm-bound in attempting to cross the Welsh mountains, took refuge in a wayside cottage, and ' Sat down for three or four hours, and translated Aldrich's *Logic*'.

We can see in this Retreat at Kingswood the beginning of a school for preachers. Here theology and logic are taught by him. Wesley with his eye ever upon the practical task of the preacher also instructs them in elocution. This course was continued, says John Wesley, about a month. Charles Wesley, writing of this happening, says : ' I spent half an hour with my brother at Kingswood, which is now very much like a College. Twenty-one boarders are there, a dozen students, his sons and pupils in the Gospel. I believe he is now laying the foundations of many generations'. In the *Journal*, under date October 26, 1756, we read : ' I began reading over with the preachers that were in town, Mr. Pike's *Philosophia Sacra*—it contains the marrow of Mr. Hutchinson's philosophy clearly and modestly proposed : but, upon a close examination I found the proofs were grievously defective. I shall never receive Mr. Hutchinson's creed, unless *ipse dixit* stands for evidence'.

John Wesley sought to teach his preachers how to reject the false as well as to welcome the true. His work at Oxford had made him an expert guide in this exercise. ' For several years,' he says, ' I was moderator in the disputations which were held six times a week at Lincoln College, Oxford. I could not avoid acquiring hereby some degree of expertness in arguing ; and especially in discerning and pointing out well covered and plausible fallacies. I have since found abundant reason to praise God for giving me this honest art. By this, when men have hedged me in by what they call demonstrations, I have been many times able to dash them in pieces ; in spite of all its covers, to touch the very point where the fallacy lay ; and it flew open in a moment'. There is another reference to Hutchinson's philosophy in the following entry : ' I read with the preachers this week the Glasgow Abridgement of Mr. Hutchinson's work, wherein the abridgers here expressed, with surprising exactness, not only his sense, but his very spirit. But in truth I cannot admire either ; nay, I admire his hypotheses less and less, as I see that the whole is unsupported by Scripture. Very ingenious, but quite precarious '. It is an interesting picture of the Oxford Don showing to his preachers the weak points in Hutchinson's armour, telling them how they can pierce his defences, and proving its inconstancy with Scripture. We must remember that Wesley was attacking a foe who at that time was modern, and was enjoying a considerable vogue. He taught his preachers to detect the fallacies of certain thinkers of that age. He tried to train them to cross swords with the modern opponents of the Christian faith.

John Wesley—as we are aware—founded an Orphan House at Newcastle, but it is not so well known that it was ' the first institution in which young Methodist preachers received instructions for the efficient discharge of their ministerial duties '. It is true that Wesley said, ' I would throw away all libraries rather than be guilty of the loss of one soul '. But he certainly did not feel that there was any incompatibility betwixt learning and zeal. He commanded his preachers to

> ' Read the most useful books, and that regularly, and constantly, steadily spend all the mornings in this employ, or, at least, five hours in the four and twenty. " But I read only the Bible ". Then you ought to teach others to read only the Bible, and by parity of reason, to hear only the Bible. But if so, you need preach no more. Just so, said George Bell. What is the fruit ? Why, now he neither reads the Bible, nor anything else. This is rank enthusiasm. If you read no book but the Bible, you are

got above St. Paul. He wanted others too. "Bring the books", says he, "but especially the parchments". "But I have no taste for reading". Contract a taste for it by use, or return to your trade. "But I have no books". I will give each of you, as fast as you can read them, books to the value of five pounds'.

In the Minutes of the Methodist Conference for 1746, we have clearly revealed to us the way in which Wesley judged as to whether a man was called to preach. His tests were: the man must know in Whom he has believed; he must have gifts (as well as grace) for the work; and through the preacher's ministry others should receive a clear and lasting sense of the love of God. 'The Minutes' say, 'as long as these three marks undeniably concur in any, we allow him to be called to preach'. A question is asked at this Conference, 'In what light should our assistants consider themselves?' The answer is, 'As learners rather than teachers; as young students at the University; for whom, therefore, a method of study is expedient in the highest degree'. The next question is, 'What method would you advise them to?' The answer is, 'We would advise them (1) always to rise at four. (2) From four to five in the morning, and from five to six in the evening, partly to read the Scripture (two or three verses, or one or two chapters), partly some close, practical book of divinity. From six in the morning (allowing one hour for breakfast) to twelve, to read in order, slowly, and with much prayer'. Here Wesley gives a list of books dealing with Theology, History, New Testament study. We see that seven hours a day were to be given to devotional practice, and to study.

We believe that Wesley stressed more than any divine of the eighteenth century the need for devotional and intellectual preparation. It is interesting to note a question asked at this Conference, 'What books should we keep for use at London, Bristol and Newcastle?'

Then follows a list of books under the headings of Divinity, Philosophy, History, Poetry, Classics, and Hebrew. It is a remarkable list of books, and it is interesting to note that at each of the three most important bases for the great campaign, Wesley placed a library for his preachers. It was said in Wesley's day that his preachers were ignorant men, but he swiftly replied to the attack—' Indeed, in the one thing which they profess to know they are not ignorant men. I trust there is not one of them who is not able to go through an examination in substantial, practical, experimental divinity, as few of our candidates for holy orders, even in our Universities (I speak it with sorrow, and shame, and in tender tone) are able to do '.

In 1763, Dr. Rutherforth, a fellow of the Royal Society and Regius Professor of Divinity at Cambridge, had attacked the Methodists, and said they considered ' that human learning was rather an impediment than other-wise '. Wesley replied, and pointed to his ' Sermons addressed to the Clergy ' ; to the establishment of Kings-wood School ; and to the fact that, though his preachers did not profess to know the languages and philosophy, yet some of them understood both one and the other better than the greater part of his pupils at the University. In the following quotation from this ' Reply ' we see that while Wesley realizes that Education is of the highest importance, he places first things first. ' What I believe concerning learning is this—that it is highly expedient for a guide of souls, but not absolutely neces-sary. What I believe to be absolutely necessary is a faith unfeigned, the love of God and our neighbour, a burning zeal for the advancement of Christ's Kingdom, with a heart and life wholly devoted to God. These I judge to be necessary in the highest degree ; next to these a competent knowledge of Scripture, a sound understand-ing, a tolerable utterance, and a willingness to be as the filth and off-scouring of the world.'

It surely is obvious that the man who issued, at cheap prices, the many volumes of his Christian Library, edited grammars for five languages, flooded this land with extracts from the *Journal*, cheap tracts, Appeals, and sought in every way to feed men's souls and minds, would with even greater enthusiasm desire to give to his preachers all the devotional and educational help that was possible. His preachers were also perambulating booksellers, and were expected to read the books they sold. Wesley believed in a trained ministry—and that training was a wide one. Great lessons were learned on the field of action, and also in the quiet hours of study—which Wesley enforced upon his preachers as far as he was able. In 1775, John Fletcher, instigated by Joseph Benson, wrote a remarkable letter to Wesley proposing that Kingswood School should be appropriated (1) for the education of the Christian ministers, (2) to provide a home for Worn-out ministers, and for the training of Candidates, who should be ordained preferably by Bishops, but if this source failed, they were to be ordained non-episcopally. Fletcher dreamed of the formation of a Methodist Church of England ; but his dream remained a dream.

In the band of men whom we call the Early Methodist Preachers there were notable examples of men of evangelical zeal and much sound knowledge. Thomas Walsh, of intrepid heroism and passionate zeal, of whom it was said that the sword was too sharp for the scabbard, was a man of great scholarship. Wesley said of this man, who died in his twenty-eighth year, thus making the testimony more remarkable, ' I knew a young man who was so thoroughly acquainted with the Bible, that if he was questioned concerning any Hebrew word in the Old, or any Greek word in the New Testament, he would tell, after a little pause, not only how often the one or the other occurred in the Bible, but also what it meant in every place. His name was Thomas Walsh. Such a master of Biblical knowledge I never saw before, and never expect to see again '. Three men who were amongst Wesley's itinerating preachers wrote Commentaries on the whole of the Bible—Dr. Adam Clarke, Joseph Benson, and Joseph Sutcliffe. Francis Asbury, notwithstanding his apostolic journeyings, became—as Dr. Bett says— ' thoroughly proficient in Latin, Greek, and Hebrew '.

The early Methodist preachers all looked up to Wesley as their father in God. It was not possible for them to work with him without catching some of his infectious zeal for knowledge. Dr. Bett shows in his most informing lecture, *The Early Methodist Preachers*, that many of Wesley's helpers were drawn from those who had received a grammar-school education. These men, amidst long journeys and arduous evangelical campaigns, steadily added to their knowledge, and became, especially in Biblical knowledge, men of sound learning. Others of the preachers had not the advantages of a grammar-school education, but few of them believed that ignorance was the key to evangelical success. In every way possible they sought to increase their knowledge, and they devoted themselves with great zeal to study, especially to that of the Scriptures. We believe that it was part of the early Methodist tradition for the preachers to consider time as a sacred gift, and to use the time which was not given to specifically evangelistic work in such a way as to prepare themselves by prayer and study for the work of the ministry. It has been my lot often to pass through the Yorkshire town of Birstall, and I never do so without paying homage to that great fellow-worker of Wesley's—John Nelson. He was a stone-mason, and through the ministry of Wesley was soundly converted to God, and became one of the greatest of the itinerating preachers. In the grounds of the Birstall Methodist chapel can still be seen the study, a little one-roomed building, which John Nelson built. Here he prayed, and here he studied. Such things are an allegory, and testify to the fact that this early band of men, being denied the privileges of a theological training in a semi-nary, found other ways of winning those privileges which the exigencies of their time and age had denied them. They could not all, as John Nelson, build a study with stones from some local quarry, but they were resourceful in finding places where in stillness and quiet they added unto faith—knowledge.

CHAPTER II

THE STRUGGLE FOR A THEOLOGICAL INSTITUTION

It had not been possible in the days of Wesley to find any fixed home for the training of Methodist ministers. After his passing there was the difficult and all-absorbing task of consolidating and extending the work. This problem was tackled with courage and energy, and with great success. The days were strangely difficult, for there were many schools of thought in the Methodist Society. Some wanted to move slowly, and others urged a complete and swift severance from the Church of England. The times were too critical for the leaders to consider the foundation of a school for the young preachers. The death of Wesley synchronized with the birth of the French Revolution. Soon the nation was flung into the whirlpool of war, and there was the life and death struggle with Napoleon. Added to the difficulties which arose through this great struggle, there were the problems within the Church itself. There were fightings without, and fears within. It says much for the inherent strength of the Wesleyan community that it not only survived the great difficulties of this period, but that it steadily advanced in these days of storm and stress. Well might its people say 'What hath God wrought?' Charles Greville wrote in his diary, under date of January 1, 1832, 'Distress seems to increase hereabouts, and crime with it. Methodist and Saintship increase too'.

In 1797, the Methodist New Connexion was founded, and in 1812 the Primitive Methodist Church came into being, and the Bible Christians in 1815. Despite all the difficulties of division, of social and political disorder, the Wesleyan Methodist Church went steadily forward, and in the twenty-five years between 1790, the last year of Wesley's life, and 1815, its membership in the British Isles had grown from 71,688 to 211,063, an increase of 139,375; its number of ministers from 294 to 868. In Overseas Missions its membership had risen from 5,300 to 19,835, an increase of 14,535, and its Overseas ministers from 19 to 74. After 1815 there was great unrest in the country, and the post-war problems at the close of the Napoleonic wars were greater even than those of our own post-war days. There were no social services; there was acute poverty, and great trade depression, and a growl of discontent made all the greater by governmental oppressive measures. The young giant of the Industrial Era was waxing strong, and many were the forces arrayed against it. During these days we see the rise of the Luddites, the massacre of the innocent demonstrators at Peterloo, the rise and fierce struggle of the Chartists, and the fight for the extension of the franchise, culminating in the Reform Bill of 1832. Throughout this period Wilberforce, Granville Sharp, Clarkson, enthusiastically supported by the Methodists, were fighting for the abolition of slavery—that trade which Wesley called ' the sum of all the villainies ', and in 1834 every slave in the British Empire became free.

It was a difficult time for the Wesleyan Church, but, nevertheless, in the years from 1815–1840, her membership at home and abroad rose from 230,948 to 428,729— that is, it nearly doubled its numbers in that period. It is an amazing result—despite secessions, new Methodist movements, the swirling agitation of social reformers, and the dire distress of a large portion of the people, the Wesleyan Church advanced by leaps and bounds. With the exception of three years, each year between 1815 and 1840 reported a considerable increase. It was obvious that this rapid progress made new demands on its ministry. In the Minutes of Conference of 1800 we find the following : ' Question 14. Are the preachers' houses sufficiently provided with books, and in particular, with Commentaries on the Bible? We think not. We recommend to the Superintendents of the Circuits to speak to the members of the Quarterly and Leaders' Meetings on the subject, that such books be provided for the preachers as soon as possible; particularly Dr. Coke's *Commentary*'. It is obvious from this question and answer that the Conference was concerned about the reading of its ministers. But it was not until 1806 that it considered on a broader basis the question of the instruction of its preachers.

In the Minutes of the Conference of 1806, held at Leeds, we find that Dr. Adam Clarke was present, and responsible for the question: 'What is the decision on the plan which has been proposed for the improvement of our young preachers? Answer: Let the heads of the plan referred to be printed, and a copy sent to every preacher: that the brethren may have the opportunity of considering it maturely at their next District Meetings, and report their collective judgement concerning it to the next Conference'. In 1807 this pamphlet, which now lies before us as we write, was printed as directed by the Conference. It is entitled ' Observations on the importance of adopting a plan of Instruction for the preachers who are admitted on trial in the Methodist Connexion. Submitted to the consideration of the preachers at their ensuing District Meetings'. On the first page is the appropriate text, ' Study to shew thyself approved unto God, a workman that needeth not to be ashamed, rightly dividing the Word of Truth'. It shows that new occasions teach new duties, and that the new conditions demand changed methods. We will quote a few sentences from this little-known pamphlet. ' The (early) preachers were exactly suited to their work, and were made the blessed instruments of turning multitudes from darkness to light. Since that period a great change, it is well known, has taken place in Society at large ; and it may be fairly doubted whether God would use even such men as *our* immortal John Nelson for extensive usefulness in the present day.' The writer refers to the great increase in the sale of books, and points out, we believe rightly, that ' The Methodist preachers have been very extensive instruments in the hands of Divine Providence, in diffusing a taste for reading all over the nation, by selling the books published by Wesley and others '. The writer admits that by the foolishness of preaching men are made wise, but points out that ' not by foolish preaching are people made thus wise '. He points out that several young junior preachers have not the means to get good books : nor have they, in general, any direction as to what books to read, or how to use them.

The writer inserts a letter from the great Dr. Adam Clarke, who gave thirty years to his *Commentary* beginning and ending it upon his knees. Dr. Clarke writes from City Road Chapel (under date of June 16, 1806) and says : ' We want—God knows ! We want some kind of seminary for educating workmen for the vineyard of our God, as need not be ashamed. We need without delay to get such a place established, either at Bristol or London. The time is coming, and now is, when illiterate piety can do no more for the interest and permanency of the work of God than lettered irreligion did formerly '. He is a great example of the blending of knowledge and evangelical passion. It was said of him, ' His hearers knew that they were face to face with a messenger of God. He came before them fully dressed in the mantle of salvation. He lived the Gospel '. He died in 1832, before his dream was realized, the opening of the first Wesleyan Theological Institution, but it owed very much to his influence. He was a man of great learning, and knew twenty-one different languages. It was the fire of religion that set aflame his mind, and gave him his deep desire for knowledge. He said, ' After I found the peace of God, I learned more in one day than I could formerly in a month.   I found that religion was the gate to true learning, and they who went through their study without it had double work to do '. His portrait rightly finds a place in Didsbury, our oldest existing Methodist College, for it was largely through his advocacy that our first Theological Institution came into existence.

Although the times were out of joint, and the days were difficult, in 1833 the question of the training of the ministry came to the front, and in December 1834 the beginnings of that work were make at Hoxton. We will tell the story as briefly as possible.   We must try to place ourselves back in those years.   In 1834 our membership was 365,857, whereas in 1790 it had been 71,688. Betwixt the last year of Wesley's life and the time when the Methodist ministers decided that a certain number of Junior Preachers should have a definite theological education, its membership had risen by 294,169.   These figures are eloquent.   But they were made to speak on behalf of both sides.   Those who were opposed to the establishment of a Theological Institution could say, ' How well we have done without one.   A course of theological education will damp down the ardour of evangelical zeal '.   The other side could and did reply, ' We have now a much larger constituency, and a better educated people, and we must have trained preachers to minister to our people.   Wise training in a Theological Institution will kindle to a greater flame the evangelical zeal of its students '.

It was a difficult situation, and as we read the reports of the movement on behalf of the founding of a Theological Institution we realize that many trembled for the ark, and that those who supported the new project were most solicitous to convince the opponents of the scheme that they did not wish to start a secular academy, but a Wesleyan Theological Institution, where the first and predominant task would be to deepen the experience of students in the knowledge of the redeeming grace of Christ—and that its dominant aim would be to strengthen faith, and to add knowledge to faith.   It is clear that this was considered the *raison d'être* of the Theological Institution.   Its task was to prepare men for the Christian ministry.   Its work was essentially different from a secular academy or college—and all the early reports of the Theological Institution make it quite clear that the training given was a help, and not a hindrance, to evangelistic work.   They wrote thus, we believe, for two reasons —they were anxious to allay distrust, and to silence opponents, or rather to win them to their side—and also, they believed what they said.   For we are sure that both the supporters and opponents of the scheme were one in this, that they each wished to deepen the evangelical faith and love of the younger Wesleyan ministers.   It was at the Conference of 1834 that it was agreed that there should be a Theological Institution.   We believe that the supporters of the scheme were right—that there may be a true marriage of knowledge and zeal.

At the Conference of 1833 a Committee was appointed to provide a scheme for the education of preachers on the list of reserve.   It is necessary to point out that the original scheme was only for the training of a portion of the Wesleyan preachers.   This Committee met in the October of that year.   An elaborate report was prepared and published under the title of ' Proposals for the formation of a Literary and Theological Institution, with a design to promote the improvement of the Junior Preachers in the Methodist Connexion '.   The title is not a little stilted and top-heavy—but we know what it means.   These proposals were embodied in a series of resolutions submitted to the next Conference.   The Committee also nominated persons to fill the principal offices—those of president, house-governor, theological tutor, and classical tutor.   The Committee—in the

absence of Dr. Jabez Bunting—resolved that ' he should
be requested to allow himself to be nominated as president
of the proposed institution '. Dr. Bunting was at this
time Senior Secretary at the Mission House. It was
suggested that ' such arrangement should be made,
respecting the duties of the President of the Institution as
should be compatible with his present office of Senior
Secretary at the Mission House '. It was also proposed
that he ' should name such persons as he should think
proper for the tutorships ; to which proposal he immediately gave a peremptory and decided negative '. The
situation had become Gilbertian—too Gilbertian even
for Dr. Bunting. But it was to become more Gilbertian,
for Dr. Bunting was proposed as president and theological tutor.

Dr. Warren characterized this as ' the astounding
proposal that Dr. Bunting should not only be the President of the Institution, but also a theological tutor, and
at the same time retain the responsible and influential
office of Senior Secretary of our Foreign Missions '.
He turned to Dr. Bunting and said, ' to such an extra-
ordinary assumption of power I would never give my
consent '. Here we heartily agree with Dr. Warren, who
seems to have supported at first the scheme for the training of Methodist preachers. Soon, however, he became
its most rigorous opponent. It is not our purpose,
nor are we able, to search his motives—we can only deal
with his actions. He was certainly highly indignant. He
launched a vigorous attack upon the Conference, and
founded ' The Grand Central Association ', in November
1834, at Manchester, where he was then travelling. In
1835, owing to his so-called contumacy and determined
agitation, he was expelled from the ministry, and headed
a secession, the members of which were called Warrenites.
He shortly afterwards entered the ministry of the Church
of England. It is an unpleasant story, and marks a
difficult beginning for the Theological Institution. Dr.

Warren was certainly a litigious person. After his expulsion, he appealed to the civil courts against the Conference decision, first to the Vice-Chancellor's court, where his appeal was dismissed. Then he appealed to the Lord Chancellor, Lord Lyndhurst, and his decision was also given against Dr. Warren. It was a momentous pronouncement for Methodism, for it legally decreed that the Conference was master of its own house. We will not, however, linger upon this agitation of a hundred years ago. We wish, however, to make it quite clear that Dr. Warren was originally a strong supporter of the idea of the training of the ministry, and he wished the place of their training to be called a College, and not an Institution. His quarrel was not against the scheme, but rather against the way in which it was being planned. It was an affair of personalities rather than of policy. Despite the fierceness of this tempest, the Theological Institution scheme weathered the storm.

In 1834, the Conference received the report of the Committee. The ' Minutes ' describes the new department as ' The Wesleyan Theological Institution for the improvement of the Junior Preachers '. There was considerable opposition to the suggestions. One speaker opposed the suggested scheme for four reasons : (1) The prolongation of the enforced celibacy of probationers, (2) the proverbial dangers of College life to young men, (3) the uncertainty of beneficial results, (4) having our ministers all cast in one mould. Another speaker thought that money might be better used in supplying suitable books to young preachers. Another speaker quoted Elijah as an example of a successful though uneducated preacher. To this speaker another speaker replied by saying that ' Elijah was the great reviver, not only of religion, but of the schools of the prophets in the kingdom of the ten tribes '. A reply which illustrates the effectiveness, and also the superficiality, of the debating dialectic. After the debate, the Committee's recommendations were carried. The fears of some were allayed, when it was known that an old and experienced minister would be appointed as Governor. One member of the Conference expressed his satisfaction, and that of others, when he said that he was ' glad to find that a Governor would be appointed to look after the piety of the young men. Many errors to be deplored may thus be avoided '. The Conference then proceeded to appoint the officers. Dr. Bunting, deeply offended by the attack made upon him by Dr. Warren, refused to be nominated. Finally a resolution was moved—we give it in full, for it reveals the singularly commanding position held by Dr. Bunting in those days —' That the Conference specially and earnestly requests Dr. Bunting to take the general superintendency of the Institution, by whatever name it may be called '.

This resolution was not, however, put to the Conference, for Dr. Bunting ' promised to take the subject into serious consideration, to consult the other ministers who might be appointed as officers, and in conjunction with them to give a reply '. There were three officers of the Institution appointed at this Conference. One was Joseph Entwisle, who had twice been President. But he has a greater reason for fame than his double Presidency, for he had travelled with John Wesley. He has taken his place for ever in the following delightful story. Joseph Entwisle, as a young man of twenty, was journeying on horseback with John Wesley. In an instant, owing to the sudden fall of his horse, Entwisle made a complete somersault over the head of the animal. ' Well done, Joseph,' cried Wesley, who was then eighty-four, ' I could not have done better than that myself.'

To Mr. Entwisle was given the entire domestic charge of the Theological Institution, and the pastoral care and superintendence of the resident students. The other officer was Mr. John Hannah, who was appointed theological tutor. Dr. Bunting's words show that the above titles were purposely and carefully chosen. He said at the Conference of 1834, concerning the Institution about to be founded, ' Let it not, even in joke, be called College, nor Mr. Entwisle the Principal, nor Mr. Hannah Professor'. ' What's in a name ? ' Dr. Bunting would have replied ' Much '. *O tempora mutantur !* Two of the above titles now appear in ' The Minutes of Conference '. In conjunction with these ministers, Dr. Bunting consented to be responsible for the oversight of the Institution. The name of his office was ' set down ' in the early sittings of the Conference as ' Visitor ', and some copies of the ' stations ' were struck off with this name employed. It was, however, afterwards changed to that of ' President '. The official resolution declares : ' The Rev. Jabez Bunting is appointed to the office of President of the Institution, under such arrangements as may render his acceptance of that office convenient to himself and compatible with the retention of his present situation as Senior Secretary of the Wesleyan Missionary Society. N.B. It is not intended to attach any salary whatever to the office of President as such '. It was a strange position, for Mr. Entwisle was twelve years Dr. Bunting's senior in the ministry, and Mr. Entwisle would be called upon to receive two visits a week from his junior ' overlord '. It was an unnecessary appointment, and no one else held it after the death of Dr. Bunting.

From the inception of the Theological Institution until 1857—for twenty-two years—Dr. Bunting was its President. He never treated his office as a sinecure, but was throughout those years its chief counsellor and guide. There can be no doubt that the prestige of his name, and his commanding influence and keen enthusiasm for the work, did much to quicken the interest in the training of Wesleyan preachers. His biographer and son, T. P. Bunting, says : ' The office, as he accepted and fulfilled it, involved a very large addition to his work, especially

A COLLEGE CHAPEL.

in the early days of the great undertaking. His personal
control was active both in the building and furnishing of
the Colleges, in the arranging of the course of study, and
in all matters of administration. Statements of the accounts of local and general treasurers were sent to him
periodically and preserved. He was kept informed of all
disciplinary proceedings, and was frequently engaged in
correspondence concerning the personal interests of
individual students.' There can be no doubt that, however singular his office appears, Dr. Bunting gave
great service to the Theological Institution in its early
years. He was a man with large ideas, and those who
know the buildings and grounds of Didsbury and Richmond will realize that he brought spacious ideas into
the fashioning of our two earliest Colleges.

C

CHAPTER III

HOXTON THEOLOGICAL INSTITUTION

IMMEDIATELY after the Conference of 1834, the Committee which had decided that there was urgent need for a Theological Institution, in the same month as the Conference closed, found premises in which to begin its work. These were in Hoxton, and had been formerly occupied by the London Missionary Society for the ministerial instruction of their candidates for missionary service. Prior to this it had been the Hoxton Academy, which had taken for many years a prominent place in the work which was done in this country for ministerial education by the Dissenting Academies. Readers of John Wesley will remember his admiration for the work done by the Northampton Academy, of which the great Dr. Doddridge was the head, and where that noble divine delivered lectures to his students in Latin. Wesley visited this Academy on September 9, 1745. He says: 'It was about the hour when he (Dr. Doddridge) was accustomed to expound a portion of Scripture to the young gentlemen under his care. He desired me to take his place. It *may* be the seed was not altogether sown in vain'. In March 1746, Wesley wrote to Dr. Doddridge, and asked him to send a list of books which would be useful for young Methodist preachers. It is interesting to look through the list which Doddridge sent to Wesley. It shows how high was his opinion of the mental possibilities of Wesley's preachers. Northampton was one of many Dissenting Academies of the eighteenth century. There is little doubt that the lamp of learning was kept aflame in that century, not at the Ancient Universities, but rather in the Dissenting Academies. Samuel Wesley, the father of John Wesley, Bishop Butler, the author of *The Analogy*,

Secker, Archbishop of Canterbury, all received their training in Dissenting Academies. It is interesting to recall that at the Academy where Samuel Wesley was a student—Stoke Newington—Daniel Defoe was a student, and that another student, there at the same time, was called Cruso, the name being later immortalized in *Robinson Crusoe*.

The buildings of the old Hoxton Academy were not bought, but rented. In the *Wesleyan Methodist Magazine* of September 1834, we read that ' Since the Conference concluded, the Committee have engaged the premises lately occupied by the " Hoxton Academy ", which are admirably adapted to the purpose of the Institution, and will be fitted up with all convenient speed '. In the November 1834 issue of the *Magazine*, in an interesting article entitled ' General View of the Principles of the Wesleyan Institution ', signed by Joseph Taylor, President of the Conference, and others, we read the following: ' The requisite arrangements for the speedy commencement of operations are already in progress. Suitable premises for the house of the Institution have opportunely presented themselves, in the building formerly occupied by the " Hoxton Academy ". These will conveniently accommodate betwixt twenty and thirty Students ; and they are offered, for a term of years, at the very moderate rent of £85 ; not, of course, including the expense which it will be necessary to bestow on repairs and alterations. They are accordingly engaged, and are now in a forward state of preparation. Something is also done towards the formation of a library'. In the December 1834 issue of the *Magazine*, we read : ' We have great pleasure in announcing that the repairs and alterations of the premises at Hoxton are already nearly completed. Mr. Entwisle, the Governor, has resided there for the last week, and the house will shortly be ready for the reception of Students. According to the resolution of the last Conference, the candidates on the President's List of Reserve have been very carefully examined, and twenty of them selected for the Institution; all of them are desirous of obtaining the advantages which such an establishment promises'.

It will thus be seen that our first Theological Institution began its work in what was described as 'mean and dark surroundings at Hoxton'. The Students arrived on January 26, 1835, although the House Governor—Rev. Joseph Entwisle—went into residence in December 1834. Prior to the coming of the students to Hoxton, during the late autumn of 1834, they lodged in private residences, and classes were held in the premises of City Road Chapel. Thus the first teaching of these theological students was given with a certain beautiful fitness in the building, built by, and so dear to, John Wesley. A letter appears in the *Methodist Magazine* for January 1835, over the signature of 'An Observer'. He writes : ' The Institution is now pursuing its course with most hopeful prospect of success; but if it should ultimately fail, for want of support, the men who have been accustomed to complain that their Preachers were not acceptable, and to storm the ears of Conference by importunate applications for more efficient appointments, must in future be for ever silent on this subject. On what possible grounds a consistent member of the Wesleyan body can oppose the Theological Institution it is difficult to conjecture ? the principle of such an establishment having been recognized among them from the beginning of their existence. If it be wrong for the Conference to send thirty young men to Hoxton for literary and theological advantages, it was wrong for Mr. Wesley to send Jeremiah Brettell and Thomas Cooper, and Adam Clarke, and others, to Kingswood School for that purpose; and it was wrong for Mr. Fletcher, the holy vicar of Madeley, to connect himself, as President, with a similar Institution at Trevecca; an office which he held for many years, with the greatest advantage, and which he only resigned when subscription to the tenets of Calvinism was required as the condition of his continuance '.

It is interesting to read the early reports of the Wesleyan Theological Institution. The staff was :

> Rev. Jabez Bunting, D.D., President of the Institution.
> Rev. Joseph Entwisle, House Governor.
> Rev. John Hannah, Theological Tutor.
> Rev. Samuel Jones, A.M., Classical and Mathematical Tutor.

Mr. Jones was in the Irish ministry, and was a graduate of Trinity College, Dublin, and his services were lent by the Irish Conference to the new Institution. It is good to find that Ireland, to which country John Wesley gave such love and abundant labour, supplied one of the first batch of tutors, and to note that two Irish students were sent ' according to the original rules of the Institution, by the Irish Conference '. The first year there were fourteen students ; after the Conference of 1835 the total was twenty-seven, ten of whom were Missionary students. The first Report of the Wesleyan Theological Institution, says of the official opening : ' As it was found that by January 26, 1835, all the students could be present, and everything prepared for the regular commencement of the business of the Institution, it was agreed that a meeting for special prayer should be held on the premises, and that all the preachers resident in London, and its vicinity, should be invited to attend the Committee. On that day the meeting was accordingly held, and the inmates [sic !] of the Institution, and its objects, were solemnly commended to the blessing of Almighty God. The services were delightfully auspicious, and all who were present felt more deeply convinced than ever that the work was of God, and that therefore it would prosper.' The first report tells us of the pastoral superintendence of the Governor, Reverend Joseph Entwisle, and that the students were ' met by him in weekly class '. It says : ' The superintendence which he exercises, though firm and vigilant, is yet affectionate and paternal, and very much contributes to give to the Institution the character which the Committee knows that it already possesses, and which they trust it will possess, that of a well regulated Christian family, in which are domesticated a number of young men, candidates for the ministry, whose conduct and studies are to be continually directed, whose habits and character are to be exclusively formed, in reference to the great and solemn work to which their life is to be devoted '.

It is interesting to note that the weekly Class Meeting for students was from the first, as it has been to this day, an essential part of the life of the Wesleyan Theological Institution. The first year was a year of anxiety, but, judging from the report, gave cause for gratitude. The Report speaks of the diligence of the students in their studies, and then goes on to say : ' The Committee have every reason to believe that, while thus engaged, the students have not only guarded and maintained their personal piety, but made considerable progress in it, thus connecting those wider qualifications for the work of the ministry which are at all times indispensable, with those which, however important, are still in comparison, inferior and subordinate '. The writer is not only drawing up a report, it is obvious that he is trying to allay the fears of many that intellectual training in the Theological Institution would impair the piety of those who dwelt there. He tells us that each man had been asked to give in writing ' a brief account of his employment and feelings during his residence in the Institution '. The Report refers to this and says : ' These accounts, drawn up as they were with unaffected simplicity, evinced that while the mind was improving the heart was kept right '.

In the ' Minutes of Conference ' of 1834 was contained

the following extract : ' It is eminently desirable that the students, while in a course of preparation for circuits and missions, should be employed every Sabbath day in preaching the Gospel, and in other departments of usefulness ; and it is obvious that there are large and long-neglected districts in the Metropolis itself, and in several adjoining counties, which appear to present the best and widest field for such labours ; a field, too, which, beyond all others in this country is least supplied, in the ordinary mode, with the services of our preachers, whether itinerant or local '. We see that the students of this first year went not only to those who needed them, but to those who needed them most. ' The young men engaged in the important and truly primitive Wesleyan plan of outdoor preaching.' The report for 1835 states : ' In various parts of the Metropolis, so long as the state of the weather allowed it, the students took their stations out of doors, according to a regular plan, both at seven in the morning, and in the course of the afternoon, among the careless, and depraved, and destitute—and in some instances in the immediate neighbourhood of those pests of London, and sources of so much crime and misery, the Gin shops, testifying to all who would hear them, repentance toward God, and faith toward our Lord Jesus Christ '. Hogarth, in his vivid and terrible picture of Gin Lane, has made us familiar with the ravages of that intoxicating spirit. It is good to know that the earliest Wesleyan students sought, by the preaching of the Gospel, to win men from that tragic and devastating evil.

It is interesting to note in reading the first balance sheet that £5,610 was raised for the fund for ' preparing and furnishing the premises at Hoxton, and for purposes connected with the establishment of the Institution ', and that the amount raised for the current expenses of the first year was £2,284, and the amount expended was £1,796. After the financial report, there is a list of books which have been given to the library of Hoxton. It is an interesting list, and makes us regret that this kind of giving has now such a tiny place in Methodist benefactions. In the second report—1836—we note that the number of students has risen from fourteen to twenty-seven—ten of whom are missionary candidates—and that the gifts of subscribers come from the various districts in England, Scotland, Ireland, and from the foreign field. The fund was greatly helped by the generous giving of the ministers of the Wesleyan Church. In the accounts for 1836 there appears this item : 'Lectures at King's College £22 1s'. No other details are given as to this charge, but it shows that the Wesleyan Institution was wise enough to make use of the help of an external educational institution. This is of great interest—for it shows that in the second year of its existence the Theological Institution sought to obtain help, when necessary, outside its own walls. Our use to-day of the ancient and provincial Universities is the natural and logical development of this act of 1836.

In the financial report of the year 1838, we read : 'Board and lodging for outdoor students £209 2s'. This refers to a curious plan which was adopted for a short time—and which fortunately soon ceased to be. The students for whom room could not be found in the Institution were boarded out. We will quote the words of the report : ' They were to reside with preachers as near to the Institution as possible ; they were requested to be at the Institution at half-past six in the morning during the four or five winter months, and for the rest of the year at six, and to attend to the lectures and studies, in the same manner as though resident in the house ; after dinner they were to return to their respective lodgings, and to pursue their studies for the remainder of the day in their own rooms '.

The plan drawn up in 1834 of the course of study in the new Theological Institution was :

'As many of the following subjects as shall be found suitable and practical :

1. English Grammar—Elocution—Geography—History, Elementary Mathematics, Natural Philosophy, Logic, Philosophy.

2. Theology—Christian Evidences—Doctrines, Duties, and Institutions of Christianity—General Principles of Church Order and Government—Pastoral Theology, Methodist Polity.

3. Elements of Biblical Criticism—the best methods of critically studying the Scriptures—the interpretation of Scripture—Hebrew—Greek—and Roman Antiquities—Outlines of Ecclesiastical History.

4. Homiletics—preparation—composition—and delivery of Sermons.

5. Latin—Greek—Hebrew—sufficient to enable the Scriptures to be read in the original tongues, and to prepare them for further Biblical studies (*may* be omitted).'

They certainly meant to include all the subjects which were thought to be necessary for a student for the ministry. It is interesting to note that since 1834, while some have been omitted, only the following subjects have been added to the above list : English Literature, Sociology, Comparative Religion, Psychology, Church History and for Foreign Missionary Students elementary instruction in medicine and handicrafts. The range, however, of most of the subjects in the original scheme has been widened.

CHAPTER IV

HOXTON AND ABNEY HOUSE

THESE early reports of the first few years of the work of the Theological Institution are full of interest. A difficult experiment has been made, and there is much nervousness as to the result of it. But little by little we see that the work of the Institution, which was begun with fear and trembling, is gathering strength, and receiving a growing support from the people. As we read those old reports we are specially struck by two facts—the strong practical faith of the early Wesleyan pioneers in the work of the Theological Institution, and the way in which they related this new enterprise to the great evangelical campaign. It was a part, and an important one, of the great task of winning the world for Christ, and it was steeped in prayer. In the report of 1836, the suggestion is made that ' prayer for the blessing of God on the Institution, now a regular Wesleyan establishment, should be regularly and constantly included in the intercessory services of the Sabbath '. The report goes on to say that ' the Christian ministry depends on God, not only for its success, but also for its continuance, and therefore has the Lord Jesus thus commanded, " Pray ye therefore the Lord of the harvest that he will send forth labourers into his harvest ". ' We should like to make this double request to-day. For theological colleges can only do their best work, when the Church constantly remembers them in its prayers, and asks God to bless all their labours ; and to raise up for the ministry men called of God to proclaim the Gospel of Divine Grace.

In the early reports of 1835, –36, –37, we find that there is one regret mentioned, and we note it again and again:

it is that only a small portion of the accepted candidates for the ministry can find a place at Hoxton. The Institution Committee realizes that its work will never be truly done until all, and not a section, of the Wesleyan Ministry, receive a theological education. However, such a consummation seemed far distant. But suddenly the remote became near, for in the year 1838 the Wesleyan Church celebrated its Centenary, and acted with great foresight and generosity. They were celebrating the Centenary of a great year—May 24, 1738—when John Wesley's heart was strangely warmed, and the Evangelical Revival burst into flame. The response to the appeal was swift and splendid, and £221,939 was raised. The result was wonderful, for the money was raised, as the Centenary report says, 'in times of great commercial depression and difficulty'. But it was in the allocation of the Fund that we realize the faith and foresight of our fathers. For out of the £221,939 raised by the Centenary Fund, £71,609 was given to the Wesleyan Theological Institution and also £70,000 to Foreign Missions. The Wesleyan Church never did a more gloriously unselfish thing, nor a wiser one. We cannot refrain from mentioning *en passant* that the Centenary Fund also gave £1,000 to 'The Bible Society'; that this Fund was not finally closed until 1841, 'when further subscriptions enabled the Committee to allocate to the Theological Institution £2,000 ; to the Missionary Society a similar sum ; to the Richmond Institution £900 ; for Didsbury £300. A few further subscriptions were received, which left £1,081 in hand, subject to the balance due for printing Reports ; after which the residue was equally divided betwixt the Missionary Society and the Theological Institution'. The total sum received by the Theological Institution was about £75,300, and by the Missionary Society about £72,500. The Centenary Fund tells the story of most noble giving, and of still more noble apportionment. But we are out-running our story.

Still it was necessary so to do, in order that we might show how the small beginnings at Hoxton became the larger happenings of a few years later.

At the Conference of 1838 the Rev. Joseph Entwisle retired. He had served the Institution with great fidelity. His saintly character, long experience of the work of the Wesleyan Church, and the honoured position which he held in it—he had been a fellow-worker with Wesley, and had been twice President of the Conference —had made his work as House Governor of great help to the Institution and to its students. He was succeeded by the Rev. Richard Treffry, who had been President of the Conference in 1833. The worth of the Institution had now been proved by the good results of its work. Fears concerning it had been allayed, the Wesleyan Church had not only responded to the appeal of Hoxton, but was ready to increase its scope. Its task was to deepen the piety of the students and their evangelical zeal, and to increase their knowledge in things theological and in many kindred subjects. It had placed first things first. We will quote a few lines from an early report : ' To say that John Wesley preferred genuine piety, even when not associated with human learning, to irreligion, though adorned with human learning, is only saying that in spirit he had " sat at Jesu's feet " and heard His word. But he saw no necessity for either alternative ; and therefore he prayed himself, and by putting the words in the Hymn Book which he prepared for his Societies, he instructed them to pray :

> Unite the pair so long disjoin'd,
> Knowledge and Vital Piety :
> Learning and Holiness combined,
> And Truth and Love, let all men see
> In those whom up to Thee we give,
> Thine, wholly Thine, to die and live'.

In 1839, the Report tells of a new extension of the work of the Institution. It was obvious

that the method which had for a few years been
adopted of providing for the students who could not
find room at Hoxton, by housing them with ministers
in the locality, and bringing these students under the
discipline of the Institution, was only a temporary
method, and one that was permissible because a better
one at that time could not be found. ' This method
was commenced in 1837, was greatly extended in 1838,
and was continued in operation to the close of the
session which terminated in July 1839.' More candidates
each year were seeking admission as students of the
Institution, and it was imperative that some new and
better method of housing them should, as early as
possible, be found. It was hoped that another building
in the neighbourhood of Hoxton might be acquired, but
this being found impossible, a solution for the problem
was found by securing a building in another district.

Another problem presented itself, for not only was
more room required, but it was also realized that the work
of the tutors would be much more remunerative at
Hoxton, if the more elementary teaching were given
elsewhere. The report of the year 1839 says, ' It appeared
to the Committee an unreasonable sacrifice of the time
and energy of the Theological and Classical Tutors,
that they should be employed in imparting to young men
so unfurnished the mere elements of knowledge ; and
yet so long as they remained destitute of these essential
means of future improvement, they were unprepared to
receive, or adequately to profit by, a system of instruction
which was adapted to a more advanced class of students '.
It was, therefore, decided that what they termed ' A
Preparatory or Auxiliary Branch' should come into being.
This suggestion of the Committee was unanimously
adopted by the Conference. At this time, says the
Report of the Theological Institution, ' a spacious
residence was offered to them, in every way eligible for
our purpose. It is situate at Stoke Newington, a

beautiful and salubrious vicinity, and is well known as "Abney House".' The adjective 'salubrious' is purposely inserted—for Hoxton was found to be a most unhealthy place. Someone speaks of it as a 'rabbit warren'. The health of the students in the last year of its existence as a Theological Institution was alarming. Its work was devastated for a short time by disease, and the students had to be sent home for a period, because there was so much ill-health amongst them.

Abney House was the old home of Sir Thomas Abney, Knight and Alderman of London, and for thirty-six years Isaac Watts had dwelt in this beautiful home as the guest of Sir Thomas and Lady Abney, and in it he died, in 1748. He was of frail health, and in this home his biographer says: 'He dwelt in a family which for piety, harmony, and every virtue, was a house of God'. It was in this house that Isaac Watts said to Lady Abney, 'I came to stay in your home for a short time—and I have been your guest for more than thirty years'. To which Lady Abney made that perfect reply, which is so lovely a tribute to the character and disposition of Isaac Watts: 'Yes, and we have never had a guest whose stay seemed so short'. It was in the grounds of Abney Park—as we learn from John Wesley's *Diary*—that John and Charles Wesley and Isaac Watts met together and sang. We will—for the very joy of writing it down—give the extract in the *Diary*. 'October 4, 1738, 1.30. At Dr. Watts', conversed; 2.30, walked, singing, conversed.' We wonder what they sang. May we venture to guess that Charles Wesley suggested that they should sing 'When I survey the wondrous Cross', and that Isaac Watts demanded the singing of 'Come, O Thou Traveller unknown', and that the three great men —all small of stature—sang both hymns? Anywise, a hundred years after, Wesleyan students sang both hymns in the grounds and in the house of Abney Park. It is a cemetery now, and a great city of the dead—with a monument to Isaac Watts, and in this cemetery was buried a great adventurous son of Wesley—General William Booth. On his gravestone, under each heading : Born, Born Again—Went to glory—a date is given. There is a deep kinship betwixt these four men. Such men as Watts, John and Charles Wesley and William Booth, rejoiced in the experience of a new birth, and their passing tells of triumph and not of death.

' The Report ' says, ' The house and estate had recently been purchased by a public company with the design of appropriating its grounds to the purpose of a public Cemetery. The plans of the Company not requiring the occupation or the immediate removal of the venerable and spacious mansion, it was offered to the Committee for a term of two years only, at the annual rent of £125. It would have somewhat embarrassed the Committee had it been necessary to have engaged it for a longer or for a shorter time.' The Committee were looking forward to the time when Hoxton and Abney Park men would be housed in some larger building—'which it may be expedient to fix in the neighbourhood of London '. So Abney Park was rented for two years. It was, however, used until 1843. The Rev. John Farrar was appointed ' Tutor and Governor of the Preparatory Branch of the Institution '. We notice the title, which shows its relationship to Hoxton. Dr. Hannah of Hoxton each week delivered, at Abney Park, ' four lectures on that inspired theme, which, however important other subjects may be, is of paramount interest to every candidate for the ministerial office, the master science of the whole, Christian Theology '. In the first year of the work of the Institution in 1835, there were under fourteen students in residence. The report of 1839 tells us that there were in residence at Hoxton forty students ; at Abney Park twenty-nine ; and it goes on to say, ' The two Institutions being thus completely full, there remained ten, for whom provision was still to be made. To secure their full participation in the benefits in the several branches of education, the Committee gratefully adopted the following plan for their accommodation. Five, who are missionary candidates, were received into the houses of the missionary secretaries ; three are resident with Rev. Thomas Jackson, Ex-President of the Conference ; and two with the Rev. Dr. Hannah '. So this year there were in all seventy-nine students. It must be understood that this does not mean that all the Candidates accepted that year for the ministry were included in that number. It was the habit in those days for a Committee composed of ministers in the London District, ' assembled by the direction of the President of the Conference, to examine the Candidates who were on the President's List, and decide which of them should be sent to the Theological Institution '. In the year 1839, ' forty-seven were deemed eligible for admission into the Institution ; all of them more or less urgently requiring the aid of its instruction, and some of them indicating, by their capacity of improvement, the promise of amply repaying its advantages. Thirty-three were candidates for the ministry at Home, and fourteen for the Foreign Missions '. Notable progress had been made in the years betwixt 1835 and 1839, and nobly had the Wesleyan Church responded to the demands of the Theological Institution.

In a most interesting letter—quoted by Rev. Dr. W. T. A. Barber—we get a picture of these far-off days. It tells of overcrowding, and is written in 1840 by a student at Abney Park : ' I live with the Rev. John Farrar, who has a wife, three sons and two daughters, if I have rightly counted them, also a mother and a sister-in-law. There are twenty-five young men (students) : we sleep three in a room, which also has to serve as our study '. It sounds rather like the old story of the old woman who lived in a shoe. The writer of this same letter is ' aghast at a proposal to forbid marriage

until three years of study and four of probation are past '.
He says: ' I think that it will hardly pass next Conference.
It is making too hasty strides to Popish celibacy '.   His
prophecy has not, even after nearly a hundred years, been
fulfilled, for still there is the enforced ' Popish celibacy '
of seven years.

It is interesting to notice the subjects with which Dr.
Hannah dealt: The report says: ' He has delivered courses
of lectures on the Evidences, Doctrines, and Duties
of Christianity, on the proper use of the English Scriptures, the general principles of Biblical Interpretation,
Sacred Antiquities, and Ecclesiastical History.   He has
also had expository lectures on St. Paul's *Epistle to the
Ephesians*, a course on Popery, with lectures on various
subjects, such as Pulpit Preparation and the like.   He
has further read the Greek Testament with one of the
classes two or three times a week during a whole term,
with a design especially of rendering practical aid to the
students in the exposition of the Scriptures '.   The list of
subjects makes us gasp.   He certainly was an overworked
tutor, and yet he lived to the ripe old age of seventy-five.
He was a Theological Tutor for thirty-five years.   In
the year 1842 at London, and in 1851 at Newcastle-upon-
Tyne, he was President of the Conference, and was also
Secretary of the Conference for nine years.   The work of
Rev. Samuel Jones, A.M., also covered a wide field, for
as the report says, ' In the department of tuition assigned
to the Classical and Mathematical Tutor, Mr. Jones has
had a Hebrew class, three Greek, and three Latin classes,
one in Philosophy, one in Logic, and one in Geometry
and Algebra.   Once in each week he has also delivered
a lecture on the Physical Sciences'.   It makes one almost
giddy to read this list, for Mr. Jones lectured on Philosophy, Mathematics, Physical Sciences, and taught three
languages—Hebrew, Latin, Greek.   He was an early
Admirable Crichton of the Wesleyan Church.

Notwithstanding the wide scope of the work of Dr.

D

Hannah and Mr. Jones it was found necessary to call in the services of an additional Tutor in the English and Elementary department of instruction. But this was only a temporary arrangement, and this Tutor does not find any place amongst the regular staff either of Hoxton or Abney Park. It is interesting to note that in 1839 —owing to the gift by a Manchester friend of the President of the Institution (Dr. Jabez Bunting)—two prizes each of £5 were given for essays. One was for a student of the second or third year (originally the term of a student at the Institution was two years ; it was occasionally increased to three years) for the writing of the best essay on ' Entire Sanctification ', and the other for the writer of the best essay on the doctrine of ' The Witness of the Holy Spirit '. The subjects chosen show where the emphasis lay. We find in the report of 1838 that one of the students at Hoxton was arrested—or as the report says—' apprehended by the police '. But it was for an apostolic offence—preaching in the open air—' at an early hour on the Sabbath morning '. He was, however, soon released, bail having been provided, and the next day the case was heard by the public magistrates, and was dismissed, but not without the pleading of a barrister. It is good to read of these early students submitting to be ' more vile ', and preaching abroad at ' Shoreditch, Kennington Common (where the Wesleys and George Whitefield had so often preached), at the Elephant-and-Castle, Lambeth Marsh, and other places of public resort, or of great moral destitution. These students have nobly emulated the noble example of our Fathers in the Gospel, and crying aloud have besought men to be reconciled to God '.

By the end of the report of 1839 we realize that new momentous changes in the life and work of the Theological Institution are at hand. The great thank-offering of the Wesleyan Centenary Fund, and its noble apportionment point to the fact that the days of Hoxton and Abney

are near their end. It is good to read in the report of this
year of the gifts of the students to the Centenary Fund.
' The students of the Institution have presented, from
their very limited resources, the sum of 500 guineas to the
Centenary Fund. This is a most gratifying demonstration of their attachment to the system of Wesleyan
Methodism, and a fitting acknowledgement of their
personal obligation for its benefits.'

It was decided by the Centenary Fund that in future
there should be two Colleges, one in London, and one in
Manchester, and that the first to be erected should be the
one in the vicinity of London. The Conference decision
and grants were as follows :

> 1. For a new Institution-House and premises,
> in the vicinity of London, to accommodate about
> sixty students, £24,000.
>
> 2. For a second Institution-House, in the neigh-
> bourhood of Manchester, as soon as it shall appear
> to the Committee and Conference that the further
> extension of the benefits of the Institution has
> become necessary and practicable, £16,000.
>
> 3. For the general purpose of the Common
> Institution Fund, £15,000.
> Total Grants, £55,000.

That was the original plan, and original allocation of
money, but the grants were increased, and in the end
the Manchester Institution came into being before that of
London.

It is interesting to note that during the time in which
the Centenary Fund was raised, although such a large
proportion was allotted to the Theological Institution,
the funds of the Institution steadily grew. The expenditure, however, of the Theological Institution was,
owing to its care of many more students, increasing.
Great efforts were made, and with splendid success, to
make the Wesleyan Church realize that its future depen-

ded upon its ministry. There can be no doubt that the
leaders of the Theological Institution did all they could
to inspire the people with the sense of the central importance of the training of the ministry. It would be well
to-day if all Methodists realized the truth of these following sentences which we have culled from the report :
' The permanent welfare of the Institution is eminently
an object of Connexional interest. The character of a
religious community depends in an essential manner upon
the character of its Christian teachers. An incompetent
ministry can never produce an enlightened, holy, and
influential people. In the benefits of the Institution,
every society in Methodism will either directly or col-
laterally partake ; and from every circuit, therefore, the
Committee may in fairness expect its just proportion of
support.' We have quoted the above sayings because
they stand for a truth which we need to recall—the
responsibility for our Colleges is the responsibility of
every loyal Methodist. Their work is central to our
task of winning the world for Christ. At the end of the
report of 1839, there is a list of all the old students, who
have gone forth from Hoxton, and have received
appointments from the Conference. We will mention
two names which we notice in the list :

Year of Admission	Names	Term of Residence	Stations
1835	John Hunt	2½ years	Rewa, Fejee
1837	William Arthur	2 years	Continental India

These two names still shine brightly in the Calendar of
Methodist Saints—John Hunt, the Lincolnshire farm lad,
who with the help of another Hoxton student—James
Calvert (whose name is inadvertently omitted from the
Report)—Christianized a cannibal community in Fejee
(we retain the old spelling—it looks a little more fierce) ;
and William Arthur, whose life was an expression of his
well-known work—*The Tongue of Fire*. In 1842, amongst

the list of students leaving Hoxton, we see the name of one, who was in later years to become the greatest theologian of the Wesleyan Church—William Burt Pope. He was a student under Dr. Hannah, and twenty-seven years after entering Hoxton, succeeded him as Theological Tutor at Didsbury.

In 1840 there were sixty students under the care of the Theological Institution—thirty at Hoxton, twenty-five at Abney House, and the remaining five at the residences of Rev. Thomas Jackson and Dr. Hannah. In this report, which tells of the work at Hoxton and Abney Park, we read of the disappointment which has come to the Theological Committee in not—as yet—having been able to secure a site for a Theological College near London. We also read of their rejoicing in having secured ' very convenient and advantageous premises at Didsbury, near Manchester, for the Northern Branch of the Institution ', which is to be ready for its work in the autumn of 1842. Thus Didsbury, owing to a series of delays in the acquiring of a site near London, is the oldest existing Methodist College in this country, and probably in the world. We now pass forth into another era—for shortly Hoxton and Abney Park will cease to be, and Didsbury and Richmond will take their place, and find room for not only a portion of our accepted candidates, but for nearly all of them. Hoxton was vacated in Michaelmas of 1842. Abney Park was retained for a short time longer, until Richmond was opened in September 1843.

We have dwelt at some length on these early days—because they are of immense importance. Hoxton and Abney House tell the story of a brave effort—for they were founded in the storm amidst much criticism. There were many fears in the hearts of the faithful—and not altogether groundless and ignoble ones. The work was carried on at Hoxton in premises which were over-crowded. Some of the students, as we have noticed, lived in the houses of ministers at considerable distance from the College, and for a period the somewhat prison-like College of Hoxton was visited with an epidemic, and the College was closed. Nevertheless, the spirit of the leaders was undaunted, and they went on steadily with their work, winning the affection of their students and the support of the whole Wesleyan Church. These men worked with their eye on the future. Their first task was to train for the ministry a small portion of the accepted candidates of the Wesleyan Church. But they always looked forward to the day when all its ministers should have the inestimable benefit of a sound theological training. They began in the days of small things, but the work grew steadily. In 1839 the work was extended by the opening of Abney House as—to quote the words used at the time—' a preparatory branch of the Institution '. The fact that the Centenary Fund gave such a large proportion of its money to the Theological Institution shows how well the work had been done by these early pioneers—for, surely, it proves that they had won the enthusiastic confidence of the Wesleyan people. All honour to these brave and noble men who were the pioneers in the theological education of the sons of the Wesleyan Church. We stand silent and salute:

Rev. Dr. Jabez Bunting. President of the Institution.
Rev. Joseph Entwisle. The first House Governor.
Rev. Richard Treffry. The Second House Governor.
Rev. Dr. Thomas Hannah. The Theological Tutor.
Rev. Samuel Jones, A.M., Classical and Mathematical Tutor.
Rev. John Farrar. Tutor and Governor of Abney House.

We would also remember with loving gratitude the magnificent help given in the early days of the Institution by a noble band of helpers—both lay and ministerial. Others have laboured and we have entered into their labours.

CHAPTER V

DIDSBURY

On September 22, 1842, Didsbury College was opened. Manchester was, of course, in those days a much smaller city than it is now, but it had been for a long time a most important centre of the Wesleyan Church. It was in Manchester that Dr. Samuel Warren was stationed, and where he headed the controversy against the proposed Theological Institution. Nevertheless it was near Manchester, at Didsbury, that the first Theological Institution, built and owned by the Wesleyan Church, came into being. The Institution at Hoxton and Abney House never belonged to the Wesleyan Church, but were only rented buildings. ' A large manor house and estate were bought at Didsbury, the dwelling house formed a suitable residence for the Governor, leaving some of the larger rooms as class-rooms. To this building wings were added for a library, refectory, and lecture-room, with studies and dormitories for forty students. Besides these additions, it was indispensable that there should be a chapel, and two houses for the tutors.' All these arrangements were made, and the buildings were ready by the end of August 1842. We will give a short description, written many years ago, of some of the buildings. ' The front of the Institution is faced with stone, and presents a substantial and handsome appearance. The chapel, which stands near the Institution, towards the entrance of the grounds, is a neat brick building, in the Old English style of architecture. [We like this nomenclature—' Old English style of architecture '—We should not have known it !] It has a gallery at one end, and on each side. It contains about three hundred sittings. On either side of the chapel is a house for the residence of tutors. The religious services in the chapel are conducted every Lord's day by the Governor, tutors and students.' The old chapel is now the library, and is not only well known to Didsbury students, but also to hundreds of men who have been examined at the Northern July Committee. For many years, in this present-day library, previously the College chapel, the oral examination of Candidates for the ministry has been held.

The Rector of Didsbury, Mr. Kidd, was considerably annoyed that the Institution was soon to be opened in his parish, and wrote a pamphlet of protest. He was answered by the President of the Conference of 1841, Dr. Dixon. Rev. Luke Tyerman, who was one of the first batch of students at Didsbury, kept a diary, and recorded in it: 'The answer to Mr. Kidd's pamphlet is very severe. It seems to greatly satisfy the generality of the students'. How times change—to-day Didsbury College has no truer friend than the present Rector of Didsbury.

The day appointed for the official opening of the College was September 22, 1842. Didsbury at the time was a tiny village, and some four miles of fields separated it from Manchester. This day was a red-letter day, and Wesleyans from all over the North gathered at Didsbury to be present on the occasion. The students, who numbered thirty-six, seven of them having been transferred from Hoxton, and twenty-nine new students, were already in residence. The Service was held in the chapel, 'when the Liturgy of the Established Church was read by the Governor, Rev. Philip C. Turner, who had held the same position at Hoxton for one year, and who ceased to be Governor at the end of his first year at Didsbury, and was followed by Rev. John Bowers, who was Governor for twenty years—from 1843 to 1863, and President of the Conference in 1858'. A sermon was preached by the President of the Conference,

Dr. Thomas Hannah, who was also Didsbury's newly-appointed Theological Tutor. He was to spend twenty-five years at Didsbury. He retired in 1867, and died in the same year, and was laid to rest in the graveyard of Didsbury Parish Church, where on his tomb are inscribed the words, ' Blessed are the pure in heart, for they shall see God '. All who knew him saw that the benediction of the pure in heart was his portion. He took most appropriately as his text at the opening of Didsbury College—' One thing have I desired of the Lord, that will I seek after ; that I may dwell in the house of the Lord all the days of my life, to behold the beauty of the Lord, and to inquire in His temple'. One who was present spoke of ' the richly solemn, but animated eloquence of the preacher, and of the unction from above which attended the discourse '. He goes on to say, ' All seemed agreed to take the blessing then vouchsafed as a token of the divine approbation in the founding of the Institution, and an earnest of many future blessings to be bestowed upon the students in the establishment, and through them on the Connexion at large '. Rev. Luke Tyerman recorded in his diary the heads of Dr. Hannah's sermon: first, the Psalmist's desire ; second, why he desired ; third, its nature (1) Intense, (2) Practical. Mr. Tyerman's admiration for Dr. Hannah was seemingly unbounded. His diary contains scores of pages reporting his lectures. He says: ' Dr. Hannah is a blessed man. I believe every student feels increasingly attracted to the Doctor every succeeding day '. Here is another extract: ' I heard a blessed sermon from Dr. Hannah. Text John xiv, 2, 3. I have not experienced so much of hallowing influence under any sermon for a long time past '.

It happened nearly a hundred years ago, but that first text is still remembered by Didsbury men. As we assemble at the beginning of each new year in the Library, which was then the chapel, we recall Dr. Hannah's text, and for many years past it has been an inspiration. Those hauntingly beautiful words—' to behold the beauty of the Lord and to inquire in His temple '—never fail to inspire us, and ever tell us what is our divine task. After the service, ' the friends looked over the premises and grounds, and then the greater number of the subscribers sat down for a cold collation in the refectory '. We should now say ' a cold meal in the dining hall '—but it is the same ritual, although a different language. It was a great day. The President of the Conference (Dr. Hannah) was present—but the day was greater still because the President of the Institution (Rev. Jabez Bunting, D.D.) ' has graced the occasion by his presence. The assembly was honoured by his graciousness in kindly consenting to be present '. Such were the phrases which were used in these far-off days of Dr. Bunting. They seem strangely odd to us to-day, but there must have been a certain regal grandeur about the man, whose absence from Conference for a short time suspended its sittings, and who walked as a king amongst his contemporaries. The day was concluded by a meeting in the lecture room, and addresses were given by the President of the Conference, by the President of the Institution (Dr. Bunting), and by Rev. W. L. Thornton, M.A., Classical Tutor. Thus Didsbury—affectionately called by its sons ' The Old Ship '—was launched, and its officers were the Rev. Philip C. Turner, House Governor, Rev. Thomas Hannah, D.D., Theological Tutor, and Rev. W. L. Thornton, M.A., Classical Tutor, who for one year had occupied that post at Hoxton, and became President of the Conference in 1864 ; the Assistant Tutor being Rev. Theophilus Woolmer, who many years later was Book Steward at the Wesleyan Book Room, and its crew was composed of thirty-two students. It has sailed the seas of spiritual adventure for the last ninety-three years. It has often changed its officers, and more often its crew, but it has always been a Gospel ship.

> Whither, O splendid ship, thy white sails crowding,
> Whither away, fair rover, and what thy quest?

It is strangely difficult to talk of Didsbury, for we must speak as a lover. Besides we must leave so much out, for there are reticences here, as in love. We are well aware that Didsbury is not merely a place, it is an atmosphere, it is a tradition, it is a fellowship. It is here in Didsbury, it is in China, in India, in Africa, the West Indies, it is wherever Didsbury men are to be found. It is, as Richmond, Headingley, Hartley Victoria, Handsworth, Wesley House, a magic word. It tells of our dreams and of our vows. It is not true for us that blessed is the people who have no history. For we glory in our history of ninety-three years of evangelical witness; in our roll of honour on which are inscribed the names of the noble sons of this College; in the sacrificial service of so many who have lived for a few years within the walls of Didsbury College. We will mention a few names—it is a dangerous thing to do—for it is so easy for a reader to say, 'Why has he not mentioned X?' But we must risk all that. We will mention first Dr. Hannah, who from 1835 to 1867 was theological tutor—first at Hoxton, and then later at Hoxton and Abney Park, and then at Didsbury College. Dr. W. B. Pope said of Dr. Hannah, 'His life always seemed to me as complete and perfect a life as it was given to the lot of man to spend'. We believe that we owe more to this man's steadfast loyalty, sound learning, and courage, than our Church has realized. He began his tutorial duties in days of the storm of most violent agitation, but steadily steered the ship of the Theological Institution, and weathered the gales. In the Conference, the year after the passing of Dr. Hannah, most tender and heartfelt appreciation of his great services were voiced by two of his old students —William Arthur and William B. Pope, and also by Ebenezer Jenkins. These three bore striking testimonies to the theological learning, insight, and saintliness of

Dr. Hannah. Rev. William B. Pope (he was not yet
'Doctor') who succeeded to Dr. Hannah's position at
Didsbury in 1867, said, referring to the last months of
Dr. Hannah's life, 'Whilst looking up I beheld Elijah,
and what was I but Elisha below?' Mr. Jenkins said
that Dr. Hannah 'lived under the Cross. He also lived
before the Throne'. Surely one of Dr. Hannah's
strongest claims to greatness is that William B. Pope was
one of his students; certainly the mantle of Elijah fell
upon that young Elisha. We know an old man in
Didsbury, who as a boy went into Dr. Hannah's study,
and was blessed by the old doctor. He says: 'I still
treasure that benediction!' Was it not Dr. Dale who
said 'We have lost the power of benediction'? Certainly
Dr. Hannah had that beautiful gift of the saint!

The portraits in the hall of Didsbury tell of noble
servants of the Wesleyan Church. We often gaze at
them. Our greatest treasure is the portrait of our
Founder—John Wesley. It is the work of an artist
named Williams, and is world-famed. It is the only
portrait we have of Wesley as a young man. There is
more than a little of the likeness of Milton in this picture,
and a great deal of the cavalry leader. Surely no one
could fail to be struck by the portrait of John Dury
Geden. His face always reminds us of that of John
Keats. He has the look of a poet. We have, however,
no knowledge of his poetic gifts, but we know that he
was a great Semitic scholar. He was one of the Old
Testament revisers, and one of the most distinguished of
them. The books of the Old Testament were portioned
out to various scholars, and to Dr. Dury Geden was
given 'The Book of Job'. It was a great compliment,
and a hard task. It was a difficult piece of work. The
translation of that book long years before had driven
Martin Luther to write to Spalatin 'The translation
of Job gives us immense trouble on account of its exalted
language, which seems to suffer even more, under our

own attempts to translate it, than Job did under the consolations of his friends, and seems to prefer to lie amongst the ashes '. Dr. Geden was a great scholar, and possessed the meekness of wisdom, for he said of Dr. Pope: ' he knows as much about Eastern languages as I do '.

Be that as it may—that remark leads us to write a little of Dr. William Burt Pope, who was theological Tutor at Didsbury from 1867 to 1885, and President of the Conference in 1877. A part of his library is stored at Didsbury, but the larger portion of it went to America. It is a revelation of the width of his reading. He seemed to move with ease in the Greek, Latin, Hebrew, French, German, Spanish, and Italian, languages. It reveals the catholic mind of its original owner. We must say that it was a delight to find in this library in which there were so many mathematical, theological and philosophical works, a complete set of Molière in French. His learning was astonishingly wide. He was a hungry scholar, with a passion for knowledge. He rose each morning at five. He was the greatest systematic theologian that the Wesleyan Church has ever known, and yet he said 'I am a Mathematician first ; a Theologian second'. During the sessions of the Conference, of which he was President, he was absent for a time, and was found in some out-of-the-way vestry studying a new German book on mathematics. He was an astronomer, and the observatory bore witness that night often brought him her train of stars, and not the gift of sleep. He was a man of a rich mystic experience, and even a swift survey of his library will reveal how well he was versed in the literature of mysticism. He was a most diligent student, scorning delights and living laborious days. Dr. Scott Lidgett, who calls him ' my Master ', tells what joy came to Dr. Pope when, assisting in the drawing up of the Wesleyan Catechism, he induced the Committee in answer to the Question ' Who is God ? ' to give no abstruse, abstract reply, but to say, ' God is our Father '. Although such a strenuous scholar, he was simple, humorous, and most homely. His granddaughter, who often stayed in his home, tells us that the trees near his home at Didsbury had a rookery, and he delighted in watching with her the manœuvres of these birds, and for a number of mornings, when she came down to breakfast, she found a letter from Rook No. 1, No. 2. Of Dr. Pope, of whom he says ' He was *au fait* with everything ', Dr. Wilkinson tells how he was walking in front of the College, on a summer's day with this profound theologian, when suddenly Dr. Pope stopped, and said ' The Derby has just been run. I wonder who is the winner?' Dr. Wilkinson also tells us a story of Dr. Pope which illustrates his carefulness in judgement. When a young man, he was talking with some of the members of Dr. Pope's family, and someone made a critical remark about an absent person. Dr. Pope, who was immersed in a book, and did not seem to be listening, turned to them and said ' Remember that person is not present ', and at once went on with his reading. It is a beautiful picture, and is worth remembering. Dr. Pope came of a family, many of whose members became men of learning. One was a Lecturer at Oxford, another was a fellow Oratorian with Cardinal Newman at the Birmingham Oratory, and will live for ever through Newman's tender reference to him at the close of his *Apologia*. Dr. W. B. Pope will also live on—for he has lived until now in the memory of those who knew and loved him, and especially in the thought and service of his students : and will continue to live through the influence of his life and work, which has been passed on from his students to others.

It was our privilege to know Dr. John S. Simon, who for many years was the Governor of Didsbury College. How he loved Wesley and the Church which bore his name! How lovingly he talked of our great founder! Although his speech was on this side of idolatry, it was good to listen to his enthusiastic words. It was our privilege to meet him in his days of retirement. He was then an old man, but beautifully young in his keen enthusiasm for John Wesley, and in his study of his life and times. It was a joy to listen to him talk, and to watch the smile of triumph play about his face as he told us of some new discovery he had made concerning his hero—John Wesley. It was during these days of retirement, when an old man, that he began to write his *magnum opus*—his life of John Wesley in five volumes. All through his ministry he had been collecting his material, and now—brave soul—although an old man he sat down to his long task, which he almost finished, and gave to the world the most complete, and in many ways the best life of Wesley that has been published. His daughter—Mrs. Harrison—rightly says of her father: ' He toured the dear land of England with his hero ; and waited impatiently at many a ferry which held up the great worker in his journeys, or grieved over his plight in the mud of those terrible roads. The eighteenth century at last became more real than the twentieth. He lived with Wesley, slept with him, and almost literally died with him '. He died at the age of ninety, and spent all the years of his long retirement upon the task to which he brought such accurate knowledge and passionate love. There is something—indeed much—of the epic in this story of an old man's heroism and devotion. For twenty-seven years Rev. Dr. Waddy Moss was a Tutor at Didsbury—from 1888–1915. In 1915 he was President of the Conference. Many generations of students remember with gratitude the great debt they owe to him.

There is another name—for ever linked with Didsbury —and that is the name of James Hope Moulton. Surely all who met him must have loved him. For he was so learned, and so simple and lowly minded. He was indeed a chivalrous soul. We remember Dr. D. S.

Cairns saying to us that 'there surely was something unique in the fact that one man could be a specialist of international fame in two subjects'. He was referring to Dr. James H. Moulton's scholastic distinction in the realms of Hellenistic Greek and of Zoroastrianism. It is obvious that being so intimate with two wide fields of knowledge, other fields of less important knowledge were not explored by him. There are two stories about him that illustrate that there are limits to the knowledge of the most learned. The one tells that Dr. Moulton, solicitous for the happiness of a coming guest who was a smoker, went to a tobacconist, although a non-smoker himself, and asked the girl in the shop for cigarettes. She asked ' Which kind ? ' to which Dr. Moulton replied in his high-pitched voice : ' Are there two kinds ? ' That may be apocryphal—but some apocryphal stories must not be denied print. The other story tells of a young friend, who having become an officer, came, in the early days after the war, to see Dr. Moulton at Didsbury, and spoke of his platoon. To which Dr. Moulton replied, ' Platoon ! Yes ! That is the thing with which you cross a river, isn't it ? ' He was the whitest man I ever knew —and with a heart as tender as a mother. There was more than a little of the most knightly figure of all literature—Don Quixote—about Dr. Moulton. He would break a lance against any tyrant, and his responses to any call of chivalry were instinctive, and thus as swift as lightning. The most beautiful story of Dr. James Hope Moulton is not that which tells of his writing his *Grammar of New Testament Greek*, or his *Hibbert Lectures* on ' Zoroastrianism,' or of his rising in Conference to support an unpopular side—but is that which tells of his last moments in the Mediterranean. After the vessel on which he was journeying was torpedoed, he and others were placed in a small boat. Though worn out by weakness and exposure, he kept on rowing until strength failed him. As Dr. Rendel Harris, who was with him in his last hours,

DIDSBURY COLLEGE.

tells us, he ministered to dying Lascars, and said words of prayer for these poor Indian sailors. He died as he had lived, a servant of Jesus, and of His little ones. There will always be for me a singular and touching beauty about Didsbury, for Dr. Moulton lived, and worked, and loved here. He, this lover of peace, was a victim of war. And so was another member of the staff, Charles L. Bedale, a scholar of rare promise, a lamp too early quenched, and as the memorial in the College states 'A verray, parfait, gentil knight '.

What a story Didsbury could tell, if all her sons could speak. It could tell of mirth, youthful dreams and visions, talks far into the hours of the night—and of the morning. For many Didsbury men ' have tired the sun with talking, and sent him down the sky '. Hushed are many of their voices, and their sun has set ; and yet :

> Still are thy pleasant voices, thy nightingales awake ;
> For death he taketh all away, but them he cannot take.

The men who have passed over still are a part of Didsbury. They are not dead—they are as Maeterlinck called the dead, ' The other living '.

It was to Didsbury that the saintly and heroic John White (of Mashonaland) came as a student in 1888. It was at Didsbury that John White spent the night in prayer, when he was standing at the cross-roads, not knowing which way to take. One signpost pointed Overseas, and the other Homewards, for John White's mother was in ill-health. A student friend advised him ' to get a good night's rest, so that his mind might be clear to make a decision on the morrow '. ' No,' replied John White, ' I am spending this night with my Lord. He will not fail me nor forsake me.' In the morning John White met his friend, and said, ' It is all right. You know the text, that he who loves father and mother more than Christ is not worthy of Him. Last night my Lord assured me that since I am willing to do what He calls me

E

to do, He Himself will look after both mother and me at the same time'. The visit to Didsbury of a missionary, a son of Richmond College—the saintly David Hill— brought great blessing to John White. So here, as so often, we learn that our Colleges are not many, but one, and that they are linked to one another by prayer, and spiritual blessings. Mr. C. F. Andrews has recently written a life of John White, and thus many will now know of the work of an old Didsbury student who identified his life with the black men and women amongst whom he laboured, and whose life's work witnessed to the fact that to John White, there was neither black nor white, bond nor free, but all are one in Christ Jesus.

Still the music of the work of that man of sanity and saintliness, S. F. Collier, is heard in Didsbury, where he was a student, and his memorial is nigh at hand—for if you wish to see his monument, look around the Manchester Mission. Here talked, prayed, and studied Samuel Chadwick, a brave soul, a born fighter, and a great expository preacher, and a flaming evangelist—and is still a part of our College life. There are so many others, who have passed over, and yet are still part of Didsbury, of whom we could write: missionaries, administrators, faithful pastors, great preachers. But there is one of whom we must say a few words. Didsbury never produced a greater son than Percy Ainsworth. Our President, Rev. William C. Jackson, M.A., tells us that he and Rev. Thomas Naylor, B.A., were at school with Percy Ainsworth at Lincoln, and that the Classical master would often say of Percy Ainsworth's translations: 'A lovely version, but it's no translation'. So in those early days there rested upon his work the bloom of beauty. It was to Didsbury he came as a young student, and there that he vowed—to quote his own words—'to pay his tribute to the beautiful', and by the end of his short life he had gloriously paid his debt. We love the story of Percy Ainsworth, crossing the quadrangle at Didsbury, with a pipe in his mouth, and to his great surprise meeting the Governor, Rev. Richard Green. Percy Ainsworth walked towards the Governor, still keeping his pipe in his mouth. A strange proceeding, for in those days students were not allowed to smoke. On reaching the Governor, Ainsworth said: ' Mr. Green, I do not keep the pipe in my mouth because I wish to be insolent, but because I do not wish to be deceitful '. The remark is a mirror of the man. He was an Israelite indeed, in whom there was no guile. Never has the Wesleyan Church had a more loyal son, nor a more divine singer. His sermons were songs, and they still sing. He was a pilgrim, and had the soul of a pilgrim. He sought a city out of sight, found it, and became a citizen of it while amongst us. He then could say, and still can say : ' My citizenship is in heaven '. We find his message in those beautiful words he wrote :

> ' We are never so near the world, in the one way in which it is worth while being near it, as in those precious hours, when all but God and heaven is touched with strangeness for us ; and when the heart within us knows, as it knows nothing else, that it seeks a city out of sight.'

At thirty-six, this dreaming poet and merry saint, this dear lover, who loved serpents, and to the consternation of many kept them as pets, because nobody else seemed to love them, passed over, and all the trumpets sounded for him on the other side.

We visited lately an old minister who is nearly eighty. He was, a few years ago, a well-known figure in the Wesleyan Church. He is now old and frail. We talked to him of the old times, and of old Didsbury days. We shall never forget his saying with such deep feeling : ' I believe in the Old Ship '. The sons of Didsbury all over the world will echo his words.

.   .   .   .   .   .

' The Old Ship ' has carried during ninety-three years about 2,000 passengers, who have sought to be true to its motto—*Quo Vadis Sequimur*. There have been comings and goings, meetings and separations—some still sail the high seas of life, and some have reached port. But some day all the ship's company will meet again. For

> There all the ship's company meet
> Who sailed with their Saviour beneath,
> With shouting each other they greet,
> And triumph o'er trouble and death.

CHAPTER VI

RICHMOND

It was, as we have shown, the original intention of the Theological Institution, helped so greatly by the Centenary Fund, to build first of all a Southern Institution at London, and then the Northern. But owing to the difficulties of acquiring a site near London, Didsbury was opened almost a year before the other proposed Institution. But it was not long before a site and Manor House were secured at Richmond. Our fathers of about a hundred years ago did things with a certain royal opulence, and we, their children, praise them for their wise generosity. They certainly planned and built in the spirit of the lines :

> Give all thou canst ; high Heaven rejects the lore
> Of nicely calculated less or more.

They bought the Manor House, and a portion of about eleven acres of the grounds of a certain Squire Williams. This old squire was a man of taste with a passion for planting rare trees, and much of the beauty of the lovely grounds of Richmond College is due to his love of trees. As one walks through the Richmond Gardens one sees trees which are quite unusual in England. We rejoice at their beauty, and while we are thus elated we ought to thank this Georgian Squire for the delight his thoughtful love has given us. We recall the counsel of an old laird in one of Sir Walter Scott's novels, who gave his son this advice : ' Plant trees, for they will grow while you are sleeping '. The old squire long years ago fell into his last sleep, but the lovely trees have grown lovelier, and his garden is, to our thinking—and we know well the lovely College gardens of Oxford—one of the loveliest in our land. The old Manor House was retained, and a

69

beautiful building, which time has made more beautiful, was erected at a cost of £11,000. On the ground floor there were arranged entrance and dining hall with lecture-rooms, on the first floor a central library and studies, on the second floor a similar number of bedrooms. In the September of 1843—a year after the opening of Didsbury —forty-one students came into residence, including a West African negro. The total accommodation provided for sixty men. The opening ceremony was on September 15, 1843. There was a breakfast for about three hundred people, and then a public meeting, whose chairman was the President of the Conference, the Rev. John Scott. The speakers were : Revs. Jabez Bunting, D.D., and James Dixon, D.D., who said that he was thunder-struck, when he found himself, a Wesleyan minister, located in this beautiful edifice, surrounded by a royal park, and near a more than royal river. He stressed the necessity for all learning to be illumined and vitalized by the love of God. He said : ' If they wished the young men they were about to train to be scholars they must keep them close to God ; if they wished them to be acute and profound thinkers, they must keep them close to the Bible ; if they wished them to be eloquent, their hearts must be filled with divine love '. In the afternoon of this day there was a public service of worship. It had been intended to hold this service in the chapel, but owing to the large number present making this impossible, it was held on the lawn. The preacher was the President of the Conference, Rev. John Scott, who took as his text Psalm iv, 3 : ' Know that the Lord hath set apart him that is godly for Himself '. The President of the Theological Institution, the Rev. Dr. Jabez Bunting, was there in all his glory, and was eager to show that the new building was not a College. This word, so innocent to us to-day, was terribly taboo in those far-off days. He was careful to give the new building its true name : ' The Richmond Institution, or, more diffusely, the Richmond

Branch of the Wesleyan Theological Institution '. The staff consisted of the Rev. Philip C. Turner, House Governor, the Rev. Thomas Jackson, Theological Tutor, an unrivalled authority on Methodist history, great and small, and a stalwart defender of the faith, and the Rev. John Farrar, who had been Tutor and Governor of the preparatory branch of the Institution at Abney Park, was the Classical Tutor.

Thus began the history of what we all call to-day—Richmond College. It has had a great record, and has had a special connexion with work overseas. In 1863, the Wesleyan Missionary Society, in honour of its jubilee, raised a fund of £180,000. It was suggested that the Missionary Society should erect a special College for the training of missionaries. This, however, fortunately was not done, but instead £37,500 was set aside to purchase the whole of the Richmond estate for that purpose. From 1868 until 1885 only missionary students were received. It was owing to the rebellion of many against this system—first made vociferous by one of Richmond's greatest sons, Hugh Price Hughes—that this thoroughly bad system of segregation came to an end. The College, until very recently, belonged to the Missionary Society, but has now been transferred to the Ministerial Training Committee. Richmond's note is still missionary, and it has a noble missionary tradition. In the entrance hall there is the board on which are inscribed the names of the men who have died on the field. These are indeed ' Rolls of Honour '. Here dwelt David Hill, that noble Franciscan, who became a Chinaman to win Chinamen to Christ, and who, when offered a post by the Government of that country, declined it—for he knew greater honours and joys, saying :

> Happy, if with my latest breath
> I may but gasp His name ;
> Preach Him to all, and cry in death :
> Behold, behold, the Lamb !

Here dwelt Josiah Hudson, the apostle of Mysore, and in this College the fires of his love were kindled into a flame. Here dwelt also William Goudie, a man of apostolic life, tireless in toil for the Kingdom of Christ, both in India and at home. Here also W. Arthur Cornaby was a student, a man who by his life and work revealed the glory of missionary labour inspired by a life of prayer. Here for two years lived William H. Findlay, as Assistant Tutor, then gave noble service to India, and later became one of our Foreign Missionary Secretaries, and inspired thousands with his flaming zeal and splendid vision. There was something apostolic in his missionary passion. We know what we are writing about, for his spell fell on us. We shall never forget how in later days at Swanwick, he spoke to a small group in room Z, with incandescent passion of the love of Jesus for the world. Suddenly we forgot the speaker, and we gazed in silence and wonder at the Risen Lord, who appeared so vividly amongst us as *Salvator Mundi*. It was an unforgettable experience, and it lives with us through the years. Here, too, dwelt for three years as Assistant Tutor, F. W. Kellett, Fellow of Sidney Sussex, Cambridge. He was a most brilliant young historian, a man who had won high University honours, and to whom the greatest academic honours would have come, if he had remained in England. But he could say to all who sought to dissuade him from going across the seas to preach the Gospel in distant lands :

> I hear a voice you cannot hear,
>   Which bids me not to stay ;
> I see a hand you cannot see,
>   Which beckons me away.

He became a missionary in India, and died there, in the eighteenth year of his ministry, and passed over with the name of Jesus upon his lips, saying, ' Jesus: I have tried '. He not only ' tried ', he also triumphed, and offered up service and sacrifice well-pleasing unto God.

RICHMOND COLLEGE.

There is a beautiful link betwixt Hoxton and Richmond which binds together the life and work of these two London Colleges. In the Hall of Richmond College there is a brass tablet on which are the words :

' In Memory of
JAMES CALVERT
Student of Hoxton, September 1837 to 1838
Twenty Two Years Missionary in Fiji
Born January 3, 1813. Died March 8, 1892.

Also in Memory of
JOHN HUNT
Student at Hoxton, Sept. 1835 to Feb. 1838
Ten Years Missionary in Fiji
Born June 13, 1812. Died October 4, 1848.
They held not their life as dear unto themselves so that they might testify the Gospel of the Grace of God.'

Richmond was baptized into the spirit of these two noble pioneers, and it is in the fitness of things that this record should be placed in a London college which has been so true to the noble tradition of these two great saints and missionary heroes of Hoxton, and should thus link itself with Hoxton. We recall with silent reverence the sons of this College, who found their last earthly resting place, in and about the eighteen-seventies, in West Africa, the white-man's grave. Richmond is indeed baptized unto the dead. It is a burning bush which cannot be consumed, and its flame tells of a ' flambeau éternel '. Hundreds of Richmond men, going forth into the lands beyond the seas, have added to its flame, and we can say with Bunyan that the ' fire doth burn higher and hotter '.

It was here that there came as a young man in 1858 W. F. Moulton, as Assistant Tutor, and occupied that post for the incredibly long period of nine years. It was not only a great compliment to the young scholar, but also a wise and fruitful choice of the Richmond authorities.

For why should they say ' Farewell ' to a man who was, even then, one of the greatest scholars of his day ? At the end of nine years as Assistant Tutor, he became Classical Tutor, an office that he held for five years (until 1873), when he left to found, and to be the first Headmaster of Leys School, Cambridge. We just remember him, and recall how the simple beauty of his faith, and the great scholarship of this man inspired us. It might have been said of him, as Oliver Goldsmith said of another schoolmaster :

> And still they gazed, and still the wonder grew
> That one small head should carry all he knew.

We remember one of his old students at Richmond, who became an Indian missionary, and who had a most tender love for Dr. W. F. Moulton, telling us that while he was in India Dr. W. F. Moulton died, and that on his return to England, he went to Wesley's Chapel, London, and stood before the tablet to his memory which had been erected in that chapel, and when he saw the three words in Greek which had been placed there, he wept at the beautiful fitness of the words chosen—' in meekness of wisdom '. Never did the Wesleyan Church have a greater scholar—and never a more humble one. His scholarship was equalled by one who bore the same name —by his brilliant son, James Hope Moulton. It was at Richmond that Dr. W. F. Moulton edited *Winer's Grammar*, which was superseded in this country when Dr. James Hope Moulton published a *Greek Grammar* (now being completed by Dr. W. F. Howard), and thus put his father's book out of date. How Dr. W. F. Moulton would have rejoiced in this—had he but known ! But who will say that he did not ? The book was published in 1870 and was dedicated to Dr. C. J. Ellicott, Bishop of Gloucester and Bristol, to whose labours and encouragement he owed so much. On the first page, with characteristic modesty, Dr. Moulton wrote ' Translated from the German with large additions and full indices '. But it was far more than a translation. It was, in many ways, an original work, and has upon it the stamp of Dr. Moulton. But with humility, having done a great piece of work, he sought, and to a great degree successfully, to hide his name behind that of Winer. It is good to remember that this great scholar—the fellow scholar and intimate friend of Bishops Westcott and Lightfoot, and of Dr. Hort—was so closely connected with Richmond. His name to-day is probably best known through the *Concordance to the Greek Testament*. It is interesting to recall that this work, which was first published in 1897, and has been ever since, and is to-day, an indispensable work for New Testament scholars, was edited by Dr. W. F. Moulton, and Dr. Alfred S. Geden, and that the prefaces are written from Richmond College and from Cambridge, for at that time Dr. Moulton was Headmaster of Leys School, and Dr. Geden was Tutor at Richmond in Biblical Literature, Exegesis, and Classics. We must not forget that Richmond had much to do with two of the most important books for the study of the New Testament—Moulton's edition of *Winer's Grammar*, and *Moulton and Geden's Concordance to the Greek New Testament*. For nearly twenty years—1885-1904—Dr. J. Agar Beet was Theological Tutor at Richmond, where he endeared himself to generations of students by his intellectual honesty, his illuminating scholarship, and his inspiring exposition. Many can still hear him refer to ' my *Romans* ', and remember his eager enthusiasm as he spoke of some new use of a Greek preposition or a final particle.

It is impossible in writing even a short sketch of Richmond College to omit the name of the mightiest orator of the Wesleyan Church—Dr. Morley Punshon, or that of Dr. Parkes Cadman, who has for many years been one of the foremost religious leaders in the United States, or of that brilliant cavalry leader—Hugh Price Hughes.

In the year 1865 he was accepted as a candidate for the ministry, and was sent to Richmond College, where he remained for four years. He spent most of his time in reading for a degree, and at the end of his student-days obtained the B.A. (London). But the course of such a man as Mr. Hughes could not possibly be uneventful, and twice he was the centre of a storm—once when he sought to further the Liberation Society in a part of its work, and came in severe collision with some of the Wesleyan authorities, and again when he opposed the leaders of his Church, protesting against their action in seeking to make Richmond a College for none but missionaries and to transfer to Headingley (which was to be opened in 1868) all the students who were intended for Home work. Hugh Price Hughes attacked this scheme with all the fiery ardour of his Celtic passion, and declared at the students' missionary meeting his fierce opposition to the decree of Conference. We must remember that the year was 1868, and he was only a youth, and that then the Conference was almost as sacred as 'The Ark'. At the meeting was one who was Theological Tutor, had been President in 1863, and was to be again President in 1881. We must keep our eyes on these two—if we are to recapture the atmosphere of this meeting. We watch the young orator, as with that strangely resonant voice he denounces with fiery eloquence what the Conference has decreed—and actually says (mark the date—1868 !): 'Even the decisions of the Conference are not infallible'. Dr. Osborn was sitting in the front row, and it says much for his robust health that he did not die on the spot. He was now—Jabez Bunting had died ten years before—the chief guardian and leader of the Conference, a position he had won by his statesmanship and great power in debate, and by his preaching, mighty in the style of his day. He was the father of the new policy with regard to Richmond. 'Dr. Osborn'—as the writer of *The Life of Hugh Price Hughes* says—'unfortunately took my father's expression of the general criticism as a species of personal insult, though no such reflection was intended. He was deeply chagrined, and wished to punish the offender by putting him back two years'. It is a delight to remember that the defender of the young and fiery speaker was Dr. Moulton. Dr. Moulton had a great regard for this young student, and Mr. Hughes almost worshipped Dr. Moulton. It all seems now a storm in a tiny tea-cup—but it was our Prince Rupert's first rush across the plain of battle, and it was to be followed by many more dashing and victorious charges. Dr. Osborn was wrong and Mr. Hughes was right, and seventeen years later—in 1885—the Conference endorsed the advice contained in his speech. Thirty years after that revolutionary speech Mr. Hughes became President of the Conference. He brought something new into Richmond, with his straw hat and his blue coat, his challenging gift of debating, his strange blend of Conservative and Radical views—for in those days he took his ale as most of the students did, and poured out the lava of his scorn upon those who banded themselves together as abstainers, dubbing them by the title, 'The Insane Society'. This great evangelist of later years was, when a student dubious, yea scornful, about revivalistic work, and believed in a message which was intellectual and appealed to the mind. He was to change much, but the student was the father of the man. In his Richmond days the fires were burning which were later to leap into a flame which brought fire and glow to the Wesleyan Church, and to many beyond its borders. He always loved Richmond, for here mental opportunities came to him which he eagerly seized ; here love came to him in the meeting of the one whom he first met as the Governor's daughter, who became his wife and fellow-worker through the years of his ministry, and who is still with us in all the candid beauty of her love and service.

Richmond has made many great gifts to the Church at large, and all her sons give to her a tender love and a deep loyalty. But two of her gifts which she has given to us stand out pre-eminently. She has had the honour through her peculiar history of giving the largest number of missionaries for the work overseas, who, for the love of Jesus, joyously have hazarded their lives, and also laid them down, on all our missionary fields. She also will ever be linked with the Forward Movement in the Home work of the Wesleyan Church, for she can proudly claim as one of her noblest sons, Hugh Price Hughes, who preached with such power a social Gospel, which claimed every department of life for Jesus Christ. Here, as at all our Colleges the students while in residence, take part in Mission work, and evangelical campaigns, and their studies are never isolated from the great missionary task—at home and overseas. Richmond occupies a peculiar two-fold tradition : pioneer in Overseas Missionary work, and also in Home Missionary labours. May her students continue to follow the trail which has been so daringly blazed out for them by her sons of former days !

CHAPTER VII

HEADINGLEY

In 1863 the Jubilee Fund of the Missionary Society raised £180,000, and as we have already noted, the Foreign Missionary Society with a part of the money from this Fund bought Richmond College. In 1868 it was decided by the Conference that Richmond should be used for Foreign Missionary students only. This system lasted until 1885, but after that date the Missionary students went to the various colleges. It was largely owing to the buying of the Richmond Theological Institution by the Foreign Missionary Society that Headingley came into being. £17,000 was granted by the Conference from this purchase-money for the erection of the new College. The Theological Institution Report for 1868, in showing the amount of money in hand for the establishing of Headingley, refers to this grant by the Conference. ' Donations were promised on the opening day of the Institution at Headingley to the extent of about £800, making with the sum of £1,788 contributed at the laying of the foundation stone in May 1867, about £2,588. From the amount realized by the sale of the Richmond premises to the Missionary Society, the Conference granted £12,000 for the erection of the College, and also £5,000 for the building of two Tutors' houses, and for the suitable furnishing of the College and the three residences. To complete the whole scheme, as well as to provide for the purchase of a library, a further sum will be required.'

It is interesting to note that the burden of the remaining debt was placed upon the Headingley Committee—permission being given to them ' to solicit subscriptions in the Leeds, Halifax and Bradford, Sheffield, Hull, York,

Whitby and Darlington, and Newcastle Districts, and it is fervently hoped that a sum of money may be raised sufficient to free the premises from debt before the next Conference '. We note that the task of raising the money, after the Conference grants had been made, was entrusted to the districts of Yorkshire, and the North East section of England. The whole cost of this new Theological Institution was £28,613, and owing to the liberality of its supporters, within one year of its opening it was freed from debt. *En passant* we will note here that ' £37,500 was paid to the Theological Institution Fund on the transfer of the Richmond Institution to the Wesleyan Missionary Society '. The Report of 1869 says that, ' besides the £17,000 given to Headingley, £7,452 8s. was paid to the local treasurers of Didsbury for the enlargement of that Institution, and £7,726 os. 5d. reserved, funded, for the erection of an Institution in the Midland District '. Our fathers were looking ahead, and had as early as 1869 set aside money for the erection of a College in the Midlands, but it was not until 1881 that the Midland Institution was opened at Handsworth, Birmingham.

The stone-laying ceremony at Headingley was on May 30, 1867. The foundation stone was laid by Isaac Holden, Esq., M.P. On Friday, September 25, 1868, the new Institution was opened. As we study the progress of our Theological Institution, we are amazed at the swiftness of its growth. Here is the record :

> 1835 Hoxton opened.
> 1839 Abney House.
> 1842 Didsbury.
> 1843 Richmond.
> 1868 Headingley.

In thirty-three years the Wesleyan Church had opened five Theological Institutions, and the time would have been much shorter, if there had not been the desolating catastrophe of the 1849 agitation—when the Wesleyan

HEADINGLEY COLLEGE.

Church lost 100,000 members. It is true that two of these Institutions had been incorporated into new ones, but there were within that period these five ventures of faith. The Midland Institution was also suggested by Mr. H. H. Fowler (afterwards Lord Wolverhampton), four years before the erection of Headingley, though it was not opened until 1881. These Early Victorians are often despised by their great grandchildren—but our history clearly shows their mighty faith and their splendid generosity. They did their work in days of great unrest and difficulty, and reveal themselves as men of high courage and faith. It was a hard task—for they determined to give to a Church, which had no place of training for its ministers, theological institutions in which all the sons of the Wesleyan Church should be given the best training possible for the work of the ministry. They could not do it all at once—but they never lost sight of their goal—and by the grace of God, and mighty faith, they almost reached it. Theirs was the faith that

> Laughs at impossibilities,
> And cries, It shall be done !

Headingley was the first of our theological buildings to be erected in entirety—both Didsbury and Richmond taking over certain buildings and incorporating them in the new Institution. On the opening day of Headingley, Divine Worship was conducted in the morning by the President of the Conference, Rev. S. Romilly Hall (who had been a student at Hoxton in 1835). His text was John xvi, 14, ' He shall glorify Me '. After this service there was a public meeting presided over by the President. The Rev. John Farrar, the Secretary of the Conference and the treasurer of the Institution, reported that the students and tutors were already in residence. The chief speech was that of the venerable Thomas Jackson. He was a very old man, and had been for sixty-four years a

F

Wesleyan minister. He was twice President, and from 1842-1860 was Theological Tutor at Richmond. The Rev. Dr. E. E. Jenkins said of him at this meeting: ' Mr. Jackson is our dear father, standing between two worlds, with the shadows of one upon him on this side, and the blessed luminous light of the other upon him on the other side '. Mr. Jackson said : ' I could not resist the invitation to come to the opening of Headingley Institution, for I wished to see the commencement of another Institution before I go the way of all earth. The institutions of Methodism have ever been dear to me. To find these institutions increasing is my delight and joy '. He gave a speech of reminiscences, telling of John Hannah ; of John Scott, of whom he said : ' He was a man of powerful intellect, great kindness of heart, and more than ordinary practical wisdom. I miss that man ' ; of John Newton, Jabez Bunting, and Richard Watson. He concluded by saying : ' May the men of this generation surpass the men of the former ' !

The next speaker was the Rev. Dr. Jenkins, who pointed out that Adam Clarke and Joseph Benson—both referred to by Mr. Jackson—were illustrious proofs of the fact that the most efficient training need not interfere with the simplicity and piety, or with the fervour and passion of preaching. Methodism is strong in these days because of the theological unity of the ministry, and nothing would tend so much to preserve that unity as the multiplication of institutions of that kind. He hoped they would have not three, but half a dozen. He trusted that they would have one in Birmingham soon. Rev. John Lomas also spoke. He said : ' I think that one of the worst things that could be done would be to raise up a clerical sect, to produce a special ministerial caste. That would be one of the worst things that could happen. Unless the result of training made the students, I will not say better than their forefathers, but unless it secured in them the spirit that created Methodism, these

Institutions would be of no value. The spirit that created ancient Methodism was a spirit that shut out everything incompatible with an exclusive and thorough devotedness to the great religious purposes of Christianity. The great task of the Theological Institution was to perpetuate the spirit of genuine and earnest evangelical piety'. There was at this meeting considerable enthusiasm. The day commenced with the opening of Headingley Theological Institution ; it closed with a financial love-feast at which many generous gifts were made, and at which a layman, Mr. Edmunds from Halifax, after giving £25, said : ' I am glad that we have now an Institution so near Halifax. The next thing would be to get one at Birmingham—but we must pay for this one first '. We greatly admire the zeal of a man, who at the opening of one Institution, looks forward to the next task, the opening of another.

Headingley was built to accommodate forty students— and there were that number in residence on the opening day, thirty-two having been transferred from Richmond, and the remainder were selected from the Candidates accepted by the Conference. The report of this year points out that ' The Richmond Branch to be devoted to the training of Missionary students, will be supported from the funds of the Missionary Society : this arrangement withdraws from the funds of the Institution the sum formerly paid by the Missionary Committee, and the two branches of Didsbury and Headingley must be provided for without help from the Mission House. This will deprive the Treasurers of one source of income of considerable amount '. To meet this difficulty, the Conference of 1868 had passed the following resolution : ' The Conference directs that in order to meet the deficiency of the Wesleyan Theological Institution, one Annual Collection shall be made in all our Chapels, subject to the discretion of the Superintendents ; and except in case where the Society may prefer to make two '.

The Staff at Headingley, when the Institution was opened was :

> John Farrar, Governor.
> John Lomas, Theological Tutor.
> Benjamin Hellier, Classical Tutor.
> William Stevinson, B.A., Assistant Tutor.

The first Governor of Headingley, and the two new Tutors, for years had been closely connected with the work of the Institution. John Farrar was, in 1838, a member of the Theological Institution's Committee of Management, from 1839 to 1841 was Tutor and Governor of the Abney Branch, from 1842 to 1856 was Classical Tutor at Richmond—having been President of the Conference in 1854. He was for twelve years Secretary of the Conference. After some years as Secretary of the Theological Institution Committee, in 1868 he returned to the Institution Staff as Governor of Headingley, and was elected President of the Conference for a second time in 1870. He retired from the position of Governor in 1876, and died in 1884. John Lomas, the first Theological Tutor of Headingley, who had been President of the Conference in 1853, was transferred from a similar position at Richmond, where he had been from 1861–68. Benjamin Hellier also migrated from the same Institution, where he had been Classical Tutor from 1857 to 1867. He held the post of Classical Tutor at Headingley until 1877—when he became Governor, and continued in that office until 1887. He was first introduced to the work of the Theological Institution when he had travelled eleven years, and continued in that work for thirty years, dying one year after his retirement. He was —someone said to us a short time ago—' the most saintly man I ever knew '. He was twenty years connected with Headingley, and his memory is still fragrant. He was an excellent classical scholar, and a man of ready wit. When he was dying, one of the members of his family brought him a hot-water bottle, and knowing her father's love of Greek, said: 'You cannot translate into Greek "hot-water bottle".' Swift came the merry and brilliant reply, ' τὸ πᾶν ! ' It is interesting to note that the first staff of Headingley was linked with the teaching staff of Abney House, for John Farrar had been Governor and Tutor there, and all the three members of the Staff had been Tutors at Richmond.

As one looks at the names of the Tutors who have been on the Headingley Staff, we catch sight of the name of George Stringer Rowe, who was Governor after Benjamin Hellier—from 1888 to 1903. His name can never die ; it is for ever linked to the music of his song :

> Cradled in a manger, meanly
> Laid the Son of Man His Head ;
> Sleeping His first earthly slumber
> Where the oxen had been fed.

He gave to us one of the loveliest of Christmas hymns, with its singularly haunting line

> Who have winter, but no Christmas.

In 1880, John Shaw Banks was appointed Theological Tutor at Headingley. He was a man of massive learning, one who wrestled not merely with a few books, but with libraries. He was seemingly a recluse, but he soon proved himself a man of affairs, and for many years was Chairman of the Leeds District, which office he administered with great diligence and success. In 1902 he was elected President of the Conference. He was in external appearance shaggy and uncouth, and in speech a man of most awkward gestures. But such was his moral passion that, when he spoke at some great meeting in Leeds— for he was a leading citizen—his words were as hammer blows. The sheer sincerity of his character, his great intellectual power, and the earnestness of his zeal, gave prophetic force to his words. There was more than a little of the prophet in him. He was known to two generations by his *Manual of Theology*. He was a man of deep humility, and a great defender of the Christian faith. His students, scattered over the world as they are to-day, reverence his name, which is so dear to them.

It was to Headingley that George Gillanders Findlay came in 1881 as Classical Tutor, having held from 1875 to 1881 that position at Richmond. Before this, from 1870 to 1873, he had been Assistant Tutor at Headingley. He spent forty-one years at Headingley, dying there in 1919. For forty-eight years he was, as Assistant Tutor and Tutor, connected with Richmond and Headingley. He gave a longer period of years to his task than any one else has ever done. He was a scholar and a saint. He lived for and in his work. He was a contributor to *The Expositor's Bible*, wrote the excellent commentary on 1 Corinthians in *The Expositor's Greek Testament*, and also gave to us that priceless book—*Fellowship in the Life Eternal*. He knew what he was writing about through his long study and assimilation of the Greek text of the Johannine Epistles, and through his own deep fellowship with the Divine. We will recall two memories of him. The first reminds us that at the Lincoln Conference of many years ago, we were visiting Lincoln Cathedral with James Hope Moulton. At the West End of the Cathedral we saw Dr. Findlay, seated. Dr. Moulton asked him if he were going round the Cathedral. ' No,' he said, ' I like to see the Cathedral as a whole, and to let it speak to me of Eternity as the mountains do.' Which story is an allegory of his life. The other memory is of a Conference at Cliff College, where all were asked to drop titles and dignities, and to address each other by surnames. No one, however, could do that with Dr. Scott Lidgett or Dr. Findlay. He took no part in the Conference— but through it all his presence was a benediction. One of his sons spoke. We remember him saying to us after his son's address : ' Now I can sing my *Nunc Dimittis*— Now lettest Thou Thy servant depart in peace, for mine eyes *have seen* '. His name for many is seen in the list of Presidents of the Wesleyan Conference—that is for those who can read invisible print. For many years the chair was waiting for his acceptance, but he with his beautiful modesty refused it. We remember a few of his addresses —all that we ever heard him deliver—the impression is ineffaceable—so tender, so visionful, so lit up with delicate scholarship and tender love. The Report of the Wesleyan Theological Institution for 1920, says of Dr. G. G. Findlay : ' His thought and his labours were incessant. He was not only a great scholar, but also a painstaking and inspiring teacher. The counsels he gave to the committee in times of discussion and difficulty were exceedingly valuable. Above all, saintliness of character gave an indefinable force to his personal influence. Unobtrusive, yet most affectionate, he lived with a fine sense of the presence of spiritual and eternal realities, and reverence for them marked every utterance and action of his life '.

There is another Headingley Tutor of whom we must speak. We might have made mention of him when writing on Didsbury, where he was Tutor from 1919–25. But as he was before that a Tutor at Headingley, we will tell of him here. It was our pleasure to know and to love Wilfrid J. Moulton. He was a man with a large range of gifts—mathematical, philosophical, theological, and with a wide knowledge of English literature. He had an amazing memory and knew more limericks than any man we have ever known. We have never met any one who was more at home with children—bachelor though he was, perhaps, because he was a bachelor—for bachelors have often understood them best. For a bachelor—R. L. Stevenson, wrote *The Child's Garden of Verse*, and another of that lonely brotherhood, Charles Lamb, wrote *Dream Children, A Reverie*—Wilfrid J. Moulton was a perfect children's story teller. We often watched him and listened to him, when he was amongst the bairns, and have been amazed at the swift way in which he captivated them. He was a man of affairs, and he grew in mental and spiritual stature with the years. Then suddenly he was taken from us, when his ripened powers were so much needed, but he still abides in our hearts.

It was at Headingley that William Bradfield was a student, and there he drank deep at the springs of theological learning. It is an inspiration to think of him. There was a massiveness of mind about him that is rarely seen. It was our fortune to meet him often, and every encounter with him revealed the richness of his mind, and the flame of his evangelical passion, and the beauty of his saintly character.

The name of J. Arundel Chapman is closely linked with Headingley, where he was an Assistant Tutor for two years, and Theological Tutor for the last four years of his life. He was also Assistant Tutor at Handsworth for one year, and Theological Tutor at Didsbury for five years. He was a man of sound learning, and of apostolic zeal. The evangelical message was to him life's noblest song, and he lived his life according to its music. We knew him intimately, and loved him deeply. He died in his forty-ninth year. We measure, however, his life not by its length, but by its depth. We can use of him the beautiful words: ' He, being made perfect in a short time, fulfilled a long time '. He knew the ecstasy of the Wesleyan hymns, and the lilt of their song was in his soul. He gave the best of his life's work in bringing to the younger ministers of our Church a deeper sense of fellowship in the life divine. He was Evangelist and Tutor—and the two tasks were to him not two, but one.

One year after the opening of Headingley—in 1869—John Hornabrook entered that College. He had been as a boy at Woodhouse Grove School, when Rev. John Farrar was the Governor. On coming to College, he found Mr. Farrar holding the same post at Headingley. A year later, a school-fellow of Mr. Hornabrook's—

G. G. Findlay—came as Assistant Tutor to Headingley. Of him Mr. Hornabrook says : ' At school G. G. Findlay had marched ahead of everybody '. In his last year at Headingley Mr. Hornabrook was appointed Sub-Tutor. It was of great interest to talk recently with this wise counsellor of Methodism, who entered Headingley sixty-six years ago. He recalls his days there with great pleasure, and remembers with gratitude what it gave to him—a deep interest in theological reading which still survives. All through his ministry he has kept a list of the books he has read each year. He said to me, when nine months of this year had gone, ' I have read sixty-four books already this year '. Then as now, the men of the College, in addition to their studies, gave themselves to evangelical work in Leeds, and were members of mission bands. Mr. Hornabrook can, in one sense, link himself to the beginnings of our Theological Institution work— for he remembers Dr. Hannah—the first Theological Tutor of the Wesleyan Church, who in 1835 entered upon that work at Hoxton. From 1903–10, Mr. Hornabrook was Secretary of the Conference, and was the first Head-ingley man to be appointed President of the Conference (1910). He is now in his eighty-eighth year, and it is impossible to over-estimate the debt which our Church owes to his counsel. We thank God for this wise and noble son of Headingley.

When a very young man, Dinsdale T. Young came to Headingley—with more than a little repute as ' The Boy Preacher '. The years have steadily added to his fame. He has done a remarkable work, and his twenty-two years at the Central Hall, Westminster, and the crowded congregations each Sunday, tell of his undiminished popularity. We thank God that his eye is not dim, nor his natural force abated. Long may he continue to be a preacher of the Gospel !

Two have been associated with Headingley, who have become bishops of the Anglican Church. Watts-

Ditchfield was a student for a short time there, later entered the Anglican Church, did a great work in the East End of London, and became Bishop of Chelmsford. He was a leader of the Anglican Evangelical Clergy, and always retained a great love for the Wesleyan Church —the Church of his parents, and of his early days. The other is Joseph W. Hunkin, who was for one year Assistant Tutor of Headingley, later entered the Church of England, and after some years as a Curate, a Chaplain in the Army, and University Don, became the Rector of Rugby and the Archdeacon of Coventry—and this year, Bishop of Truro; and is thus the bishop of the county of his birth. He, too, has retained the evangelical spirit, and has a deep affection for the Church of his earlier days.

A small but beautiful book—*Mr. Valiant*—was published in 1926. It tells the story of the life of a Headingley student, Arthur G. Hopkins. His name is still fragrant in the valley in Lancashire where he was a minister, and in many other places. He was born in 1891, and died in 1924. He was at Headingley from 1911–14 —then a missionary for a year and a half in the West Indies, joined the Army, and became an airman in the Holy Land—then after the War entered Circuit work. He was called upon to bear tragic pain—but he faced it like a hero. He had gained the M.C. in the War, but he won a nobler decoration in his last illness. He will be always memorable to me because of his great saying, which he spoke to a friend in his last days: ' The real thing in the ministry is the feet washing '. He lived in the light of that faith. He was a keen worker amongst boys, and was a most devoted Scout Leader. When dying, he wrote a letter to his troop of Scouts, with whom he had often camped, in which he said: ' " To die ", says Peter Pan, " will be an awfully great adventure ". So it will, just like hiking into new country. . . . It is like going to sleep in camp on a stormy night—no stars, rain, and a gusty wind. Then morning, and the storm gone. . . . Just now it's a bit rough, is the weather, for your old Scouter and pal. But before long he will quietly sleep, and when the morning comes, I'm sure it will be full of sunshine. Won't that be just lovely ! ' Arthur Hopkins was garbed in the most royal of all robes—that of a servant. He, and many others of those who have been students at Headingley, belong to this noblest of all tribes.

.   .   .   .

Headingley College was closed from 1914 to 1930. But the re-opening of it, in 1930, did not tell of a beginning unrelated to the past, but rather of the continuance of noble traditions. Her sons all over the world love her, and pray for her prosperity.

CHAPTER VIII

HANDSWORTH

WE really must henceforth write 'College' for we have grown weary of the word 'Institution'. As early as 1864 it had been suggested that there should be a Theological College in the Midlands. When Headingley College was opened two speakers made mention of a College which was to be built at Birmingham. A sum of £7,726 was voted by the Conference of 1868 towards the amount needed to erect a College in the neighbourhood of Birmingham, from the £37,500 obtained by the selling of Richmond to the Foreign Missionary Society. But it was not until 1881—thirteen years later—that Handsworth College came into being.

The Wesleyan Church during the nineteenth century, and at the beginning of the twentieth century (with the Million Guineas Fund, so triumphantly accomplished), seemed to thrive upon Financial Celebrations. The Centenary Fund of 1838—to commemorate the completion of a hundred years since Wesley launched his great campaign—raised £221,939, and out of that Fund grants were made for the establishing of the Southern College (Richmond) and the Northern College (Didsbury). In 1863 the missionary Jubilee Fund raised £180,000. In 1878 the Thanksgiving Fund purposed to raise £240,000, and reached the goal, and went farther, for more than £300,000 was raised. Out of this Fund the Conference set aside £25,000 for the Birmingham branch of the Theological Institution, and also a final grant for extinction of debt, and to supplement income—making the total grant £33,817. The Birmingham District had made the notable contribution of £25,756 to the Thanksgiving Fund, and this was the second largest contribution of the

Districts, only Liverpool with a gift of £27,586 exceeding Birmingham's total—the next highest contributions being the First London District £21,664, and Manchester £21,547.

The Fund was opened in 1878—and closed in 1883. It was inaugurated because, as the Thanksgiving Report says : ' 1878 was one of the most memorable years in the history of Wesleyan Methodism. It was the first in which ministers and laymen were associated in the decisive management of the Conference. And it closed a series of anxious years in which a most conspicuous and influential development of the ecclesiastical consti- tution of Methodism had been proposed, discussed, and accepted. That Conference was remarkable, not only as a result, and the first manifestation of the change which had taken place, but because, perhaps for the first time in ecclesiastical history, a change so great had been effected without the losing of a single minister, or the alienation of one member. Not without some fears in hearts that trembled for the ark of God, but in perfect peace, and—as its sessions progressed—in thankful and jubilant love, the Conference at Bradford commenced and completed its work '.

The President of the Conference, Rev. Dr. J. H. Rigg, took the chair at the meeting in London inaugurating the Thanksgiving Fund, and pointed to the great needs of the Wesleyan Church for better equipment. He said, with reference to the work of the Theological Institution: ' Did any one who had seriously considered the question think that the case of the Theological Institution and the training of their ministry brooked delay ? Year by year that need had been growing more imperative, more importunate ; year by year they had felt how the work of the Lord in their Circuits had been hindered and embarrassed for want of means to enlarge their Theo- logical Institution '. Richmond was now filled with students who were to be Foreign Missionaries, and both

Didsbury and Headingley were overcrowded. In the *Birmingham Daily Post* of September 1881, we read these words, ' Hidden in a leafy recess of the well-wooded district which commences near Grove Lane, Handsworth, and constitutes a pleasant border line between Birmingham and the Black Country, stands a long range of handsome buildings radiant in the glories of bright red brick and terra-cotta—as yet untouched by age '. It was thus that the reporter of this Birmingham paper described the College just completed, but as yet not opened, which we now know as Handsworth College.

The foundation-stone-laying services were held on June 9, 1880—the stones being laid by Rev. Benjamin Gregory (President of the Conference), Sir Francis Lycett, Mr. William Mewburn, Mr. Isaac Jenks, and Mr. James Wood. The total cost of the purchase of the land—an estate of seventeen and a half acres—and the erection of the College was £40,000, and on the opening day all this money had been raised ; thus the buildings were entirely freed from debt.

The College was formally opened on November 2, 1881, and the inaugural address was given by the President of the Conference—Dr. Osborn—in the Lecture Hall at 11 a.m. He said that ' sitting in the Wesleyan Conference at Sheffield, in 1834—a Conference ever memorable in their history, when it was decided to establish a Theological Institution—he could not imagine that in ten years time there would be a hundred men in training at Didsbury and Richmond, and that twenty years later Headingley would be built, and that in 1881 they would welcome a batch of students under this roof. He now saw a principle for which many had long contended practically carried out, and provision made for giving every candidate for the Wesleyan ministry the advantages of some preparatory instruction before entering on his life's work. This institution differed considerably from some others occasionally called by the same name. They differed in respect of the object of the institution. Theirs were theological institutions, and but for the theological instruction which they sought to impart to the students they would not exist at all. Although other sciences were taught, they were only taught for the sake of theology. The sacred languages, the most general discipline, the furnishing of the mind, had a direct bearing upon the highest of all knowledge, which was the knowledge of God and divine things. They did not profess to impart a complete course of secular instruction, nor even in the limited time assigned to them a complete course of theological instruction, but they professed to afford assistance to those whose lives were to be devoted to sacred duties and offices '.

Luncheon was provided in the Dining Hall, and presided over by the first Governor of Handsworth—Rev. John Hartley. At the close of the luncheon the Rev. Dr. R. W. Dale gave a most striking address, saying that he had long held the conviction that, although not by might nor power, but by God's Spirit men's hearts were won to Christ, and their lives transformed and transfigured, yet the Christian Church was never likely to retain its true position in Christendom unless it had a certain intellectual as well as a moral supremacy. In the best and noblest times of the Christian Church, since its early struggles, the times when it had been intellectually strongest had been those when its spiritual power had also been greatest. God made man—body, soul, and spirit—and those who regarded the culture of the intellectual life of man with suspicion, regarded with suspicion one of the noblest gifts of God to the human soul. The Methodist Church should endeavour to maintain unbroken that testimony to the Gospel of the Lord Jesus Christ for which Methodism came into existence, and apart from which the glory and power of Methodism must perish. Dr. Dale pleaded with power for a deeper realization by the Church of the importance

of ministerial training, and said : ' God made ministers :
He also made the grape-vine, but it depends very much
upon its training as to the quantity and the quality of the
fruit it bore. The more reverence they had for a man on
whom God's hand had been laid, and who had heard
God's voice, the more eager they should be to secure for
that man whatever human training could give, that he
might perfectly fulfil the ministry to which he had been
called '. It is fifty-four years since that speech was
given by the great Dr. Dale, and it still burns and glows.
The next speaker was Mr. H. H. Fowler, M.P. (later to be
a distinguished member of a Liberal Cabinet), of whom
The Methodist Recorder, in telling of the opening of Handsworth, says: ' In a certain sense the father of the College '.
He said that he was the first to suggest some years ago in
Conference that there should be a Midland Theological
Institution. He held that while Methodists did not
believe in a priestcraft, and were opposed to sacerdotal-
ism, they clung with unswerving tenacity to the doctrine
of a Christian ministry. They believed that men were set
apart for it by the conjoint action of the members and the
rulers of the Church. They rejoiced in the creation of
an Institution for the express purpose of aiding those
whom the Church and the individuals themselves believed
to have been divinely called to that solemn work, feeling
that they needed all the culture and training and help
that the Church could render them, in order properly
to discharge their proper function.

After the luncheon, a public meeting was held in the
Lecture Hall. Mr. Thomas Barnsley—the Treasurer of
Handsworth College—reported that the whole of the
money needed for opening the College was already
raised. Handsworth College owes much to the family of
Barnsley. Its first treasurer bore that name, and in later
years it was greatly helped by Sir John Barnsley, who was
also Treasurer of the College. The next speaker was
Rev. Dr. E. E. Jenkins, who based his address upon a

HANDSWORTH COLLEGE.

remark of Bishop Simpson's ' Methodism began with a study of the Greek Testament '. He showed that the early Methodists of Oxford set themselves to the study of the New Testament. He had very little doubt that the study of Greek led Wesley into that high experience of divine love, and to the rediscovery of the doctrine of Justification by Faith. He pleaded for a greater appreciation of the value of intellectual study, and said : ' The opposition of a century ago was the opposition of vice in an ungodly world, and of apathy in the godly world, but now, and for years to come, Christianity would have to encounter a very different class of opposition. A loud-voiced and baseless teaching could not cry down the atheism and rationalism of the present day '. The other speakers at this afternoon service were Revs. Dr. J. H. Rigg, Dr. R. Newton Young, and F. W. Macdonald.

In the evening another meeting was held. Our fathers certainly had a healthy digestion in respect of meetings. When they celebrated, they celebrated. The speakers at this meeting were Revs. Benjamin Hellier, and Dr. W. B. Pope, who said : ' All their studies would pay homage to Theology—to which tangents would be drawn from every line and from every curve. He could imagine an honest Methodist saying—indeed, he had known some who said concerning some of the subjects studied at the Colleges— " What has this to do with teaching the Gospel ? " And he should answer : " Much, everyway ". The elements of science and philosophy were of great importance to men who had to preach the Gospel in a scientific and philosophic age ; and a very small key, if well made in their best Birmingham fashion, would open a large room '.

Thus was Handsworth College opened with rejoicings, and high hopes. Its opening marked an epoch—for now in the four Colleges of Didsbury, Richmond, Headingley, and Handsworth, there was room for *all* candidates for the ministry—whether for Home or Foreign work. The first Staff at Handsworth was :

G

John Hartley, Governor.

Frederic W. Macdonald, Theological Tutor.

Robert Newton Young, D.D., Classical Tutor (President of the Conference in 1886).

William Foster, Assistant Tutor.

It is a difficult task to write of a College which came into being fifty-four years ago, for most of its sons are still alive, and we have determined—with a few exceptions, but very few—not to write of the living. Handsworth has sent forth noble sons to the Home and Overseas work, and has made a rich contribution to the Wesleyan Church. It was to Handsworth in its earliest days that a student called John Alfred Sharp came. In 1921 he was President of the Conference and for many years he was head of the Book Room, and a leading figure in the Wesleyan Church. He was a man of great natural gifts, and richness of soul. We knew him well—and are indebted to him for many kindnesses. Another of the early students of Handsworth College was John E. Wakerley. Many of us remember him with deep admiration, both for his work and character. He was a man of strong evangelical fervour, and fought nobly on the high places of the field. He was Secretary of the Conference from 1917–1921, and was elected President in 1922. W. G. Allen—who passed to his great reward this year—was a student at Handsworth. He was a remarkable man, and is known through his work in Paris, where he laboured for twenty-five years. Endowed with immense vitality, he scattered joy wherever he went. Lord Derby, who was British Ambassador in Paris, said of him : ' Everyone here knows that Mr. Allen is the most popular man in the English Colony in Paris '. He gave himself with absolute abandon to his work. He lived *in* the sorrows of the crowd of folk who came to him with their griefs—and his love and practical help brought healing to them.

We knew his work intimately, and we realize that few
ministers have won such a rich affection from their people
as W. G. Allen won from his. He was full of stories—
but the most beautiful story he ever told is that of his
own life, so full of love and gay service. He saved
hundreds from worse things than death, by fashioning
a church in the heart of Paris which became 'Home' to
so many.

It was our privilege to spend three years at Handsworth
and we recall with deep affection those days long since
past. We will—at this point—dare to speak of two for
ever linked with Handsworth—who are, we rejoice to say,
still with us Dr. W. T. Davison and Dr. J. G. Tasker,
who were both Tutors for many years at Handsworth.
Dr. Davison's life has been linked for thirty-eight years
with Wesleyan Colleges. From 1881 to 1891 he was a
Tutor at Richmond; from 1891 to 1904, Tutor at
Handsworth; from 1905 to 1920 Tutor at Richmond,
becoming Principal in 1910. He was President of the
Conference in 1901. Dr. Tasker was also Tutor at both
Richmond and Handsworth, for he was Assistant
Tutor at Richmond for seven years, Tutor there for four
years, and Tutor at Handsworth for thirty-one years.
For forty-two years he was on the Staff of either Rich-
mond or Handsworth. While at Handsworth he
occupied in turn the post of Classical Tutor, Theological
Tutor, and of Governor, and for many years was the
Principal of the College. In 1916 he was President of
the Conference.

Surely no one who was at Handsworth College in the
days of Dr. Davison can be without vivid memories of
him. His sermons still live with us. He was, indeed, a
great preacher. In his Class-room he lectured to us on
Theology, and was a most clear and incisive lecturer.
Sometimes he aroused our impatience by refusing to give
dogmatic answers to questions on certain theological
themes. It was to us in those callow days of youth

somewhat vexatious to be answered by the phrase ' Yes
and No '. For we wanted one or the other. But we
have seen since that there are many facets to truth—and
that simple answers often deceive by their simplicity.
We owe much to his breadth of outlook, and to his liberal
and catholic spirit.

When he quoted a text, he often asked a student to
look it up and read it out. We remember that on a
certain occasion a student—perhaps a little awed and
bewildered—looked in the wrong section of the Bible,
and before he had found the text, Dr. Davison said:
' Unless I am mistaken, Mr.——, you will find Habakkuk
in the Old Testament and not in the New.' To one
unhappy wight who gave as the date of the Council of
Nicaea the year 1325, he replied : 'A very good answer—
the Council of Nicaea was held only a thousand years
earlier '. We cannot refrain from quoting that brilliant
retort of Dr. Davison's to a layman who said : ' I cannot
see any good in teaching Greek to the students in our
Colleges. I was taught Greek, when I was young. It
never did me any good '. To which Dr. Davison
answered with the staccato, silencing reply: 'Obviously,
Mr. ——'. He certainly impressed us by his greatness,
and was kind, withal, and in so many ways. It is good to
recall the help and the inspiration he gave to us. We shall
never forget an evening on which Dr. Davison lectured
to us on Robert Browning. It was in a true sense a
masterpiece—and inspired us with a deep love, a love not
only for Browning, but for poetry, which has deepened
with the years, and owes much to Dr. Davison. He is
now almost ninety years old, and we take this opportunity of sending to him our gratitude and our love.

When we went to Handsworth, Mr. Tasker (he was
not then Dr.) had been there for six years. He was the
soul of graciousness and kindness. He was so approach-
able and understanding. He taught us Greek and Hebrew
—and like all good tutors while teaching one subject

taught us things outside the curriculum. He would say a few words, and suddenly a text was illumined with a new light. He had always time for us, and gave us freely that gift which is sometimes so reluctantly given. He had been for four years in Germany, at Cannstatt, where he had been in charge of our Wesleyan work there. We looked with reverence at a man who talked German like a native. He was in close touch with German theological learning, and gave us freely from his rich stores. We remember his delightful story, which he told us in those days of yore. The Germans somewhat resented the Wesleyan Mission in Germany—the home of Protestantism. One German said that he knew that the moon was not inhabited, because the Wesleyans had not a Mission station there. We owe much to Dr. Tasker, so do all Handsworth men, and so does the whole Wesleyan Church. No one else—except Dr. G. G. Findlay—has given as long a service to the training of students—forty-two years. We thank God for his long and inspiring ministry.

Another member of the Staff, when we were at Handsworth, was Dr. Thomas Allen, who was President of the Conference in 1900. He was the Governor, and a great one. He looked wiser than a man should look. He was a most sagacious man. He knew the Wesleyan Church intimately, and loved to talk of its Constitution, its leaders, and its schemes. He linked us to the Circuits, for he had been a circuit minister for many years, and a most able one. Sheffield seemed to mark the hey-day of his ministry, and we delighted to hear the oft-recurring refrain : ' When I was in Sheffield——' He was an old man, but he understood youth, and never played the part of the policeman, but was a real father in God. We have never forgotten his advice: ' When you write an angry letter, put it under your pillow, and sleep on it. In the morning you will tear it up '. He was the image of Bismarck, but he was no man of blood and iron, but one of the kindliest men we have ever known.

In those days there came to Handsworth, as Assistant Tutor, one who had been for two years in the same post at Richmond. He was tall, young, fair of countenance, and full of academic honours. He brought to us Oxford and her culture, deep devotion, and inspiring teaching. Since those days he has written his name deep in the history of Handsworth, and all over the world there are men who love his name, and reverence the beauty of his loving service. In 1899 he first came to Handsworth, and stayed for two years. Then for three years he was in circuit work, and in 1904 returned as Tutor to Handsworth, where he has been ever since—except for the period of the Great War, when he was an army chaplain in Salonika. In 1929 he was President of the Conference, and since 1925 has been Principal of Handsworth College. We will not mention his name—there is no need to do so—for his name and Handsworth are inseparably linked together. May heaven bless him, and spare him to us and to his great work for many years !

CHAPTER IX

RE-OPENING OF THREE COLLEGES—THE COMING OF WESLEY HOUSE

IN 1914, the outbreak of War soon put a stop to the work of our Theological Colleges. Some students became combatants, but most of them members of the R.A.M.C. Some of them died during the War, and each College has its Roll of Honour. The tutors went into army chaplaincy and into Circuit work; and the Colleges were closed. Richmond became the home of our Westminster Training College, Didsbury was a Red-Cross Hospital, Handsworth housed a women's organization—well known in those days as the W.A.A.C.—Headingley was taken over by the Leeds Education Committee.

The first movement after the War towards the reopening of the Colleges was in May 1919. In the spring of 1919 the work of the Wesleyan Training College was still carried on at Richmond College. At this time Dr. H. B. Workman, who was the Principal, was asked to guide the studies of a few ex-soldiers, who were accepted Candidates for the ministry. At the same time, Rev. W. J. Moulton, who had been an army chaplain, was giving guidance to a group of ex-soldier students at Didsbury, and lectured to them and helped them in their studies. Didsbury was not fully staffed until the September of 1919, when seventy-one students were there—largely ex-army men. Handsworth was opened in September 1919, with sixty-seven students, Richmond in 1920. In 1920 there were sixty-eight students at Didsbury, fifty-five students at Richmond, and sixty-nine at Handsworth. 'Most of these 192 men,' says the Report of 1921, ' had been engaged in military service, some of them having had their College course interrupted for that purpose; and it may be safely said that all of them commenced, or resumed their student life, with great gratitude and with an earnestness which was all the greater because of the tragic experience through which they had been called to pass.'

Headingley was, however, still retained by the Leeds Education authorities. The work was carried on by the three Colleges—two of which were much overcrowded. Some rearrangement as to the work of the various Colleges was made—for the dominant word after the War was reconstruction. Much careful planning had been made during the years of the War with regard to the work of the Colleges, when the War ended. Philosophy was to find a special place in the curriculum of Richmond, Hebrew and the Old Testament at Handsworth, English and the English Bible at Didsbury, and Church History at Headingley. Three-quarters of this scheme came into operation immediately after the War, the other quarter in 1930, when Headingley was reopened. There was a little alteration in the pattern, but these changes are another illustration of the well-known words: ' The more we change : the more we are the same '. The main outline of the syllabus was the same as before—the emphasis still being where it was before the War. As there were only three Colleges reopened, there were migrations of tutors from one College to another. A few changes were made in the Staff of each College, and new Tutors were appointed.

By September 1920 three Colleges had again started their work. It looked as if the work of theological training in the Wesleyan Church would be for some years carried on by three Colleges. Times were difficult, and the reopening of Headingley seemed remote. But soon, however, the Wesleyan Church was to have a distinct and most valuable addition in its work for the training of the ministry.

In 1921, a house belonging to Cheshunt College was

ENTRANCE TO WESLEY HOUSE, CAMBRIDGE.

rented, and it became the first home of our theological
work in Cambridge. It was the residence of Dr.
Maldwyn Hughes, the first Principal of this new scheme,
and the dining-room became a lecture-room, and the
drawing-room a common-room for the men. The
students lived at Cheshunt College, which could be
approached from the garden of the house of Dr. Hughes.
Our work in Cambridge in these early days was greatly
helped by the hospitality and helpfulness of Dr. Cave,
then Principal of Cheshunt College, and Mr. Johnson,
who was resident Tutor there. There were six students.
Four of these were ex-servicemen. Two of them were
Cambridge graduates, the other four represented, as
graduates, different Universities—Bangor, Manchester,
Liverpool, and Leeds. It is interesting to look through
the list of the first students of Wesley House. Thirteen
years later, in 1934, one of them was appointed Theological Tutor at Headingley. But we must tell, in brief,
the story of the genesis of this new venture. Mr.
Michael Gutteridge, a man of wealth and vision, was
anxious to help the work of training the theological
students of the Wesleyan Church. To this he gave the
munificent sum of £50,000. He decided, after consulta-
tion with his friends, that the money should be used to
found some house of theological learning for Wesleyan
students at Cambridge. He wished this to be a post-
graduate Institution. Mr. William Greenhalgh (of
Southport) decided to come to the aid of this scheme,
which he did most nobly by giving £20,000. He
believed in the proposals of Mr. Gutteridge, but hoped
that, while keeping it a College for post-graduates, room
would be found for a few students who had not already
had the privilege of a University education.

Neither of these two noble benefactors of Cambridge
had received the benefit of a University education, and
both had spent their lives in commerce, and had known
great success therein. Mr. Michael Gutteridge had

lived during the more active period of his life in Italy, where he had built up a large business. He retired and returned to England, where with beautiful modesty he made himself a servant of many good causes, spending the last two decades of his life in seeking to help forward the work of ministerial training. Mr. Greenhalgh started life as a weaver near Bolton, was most successful in business, became the President of the Local Preachers' Mutual Aid Association, and joyfully gave his generous help to the founding of Wesley House. It should be remembered that our University venture became possible through the vision and generosity of two non-university men. It was a pleasure to know both these noble sons of the Wesleyan Church, and to admire them greatly for their munificence and character. Mr. Greenhalgh did not live to see the scheme, in which he was so deeply interested, reach its fulfilment. But his dream came true. Mr. Greenhalgh as a boy was denied all the benefits of school. He was in the habit then of rising at four a.m. and throwing pebbles at the window of a fellow-villager who was a little educated, so that he might gather up some of learning's crumbs, before he went to a Lancashire mill at five a.m. There was great largeness of heart in this man, who having been denied even elementary education, sought to give a University Education to some of the ministerial students of the Church of his love.

Mr. Michael Gutteridge had the joy of living until Wesley House had been established for fourteen years. He saw the commencement of the work, when Dr. Hughes lived at Brookside, Cambridge, and the six students were housed in Cheshunt College—assembling for lectures at Brookside; he watched the new buildings rise in Jesus Lane; rejoiced at the opening of the Chapel of Wesley House; and was delighted to see Wesley House, which commenced in such a small way, establishing itself in the life of the University, and winning its way into the affections of our people. He died in May 1935

—at the age of ninety-three—having lived to see his dream come true. He not only gave £50,000 to the original fund, but also gave his thoughtful counsel and help to this home of Theological learning which he loved so much. Dr. Ritson has rightly said: 'Wesley House is the monument to Mr. and Mrs. Gutteridge. With sound instinct they saw that the key men in Church life are the ministers. They had great ideas and ideals of the Christian ministry. Instead of criticizing those who fell short, they said, " We will do all in our power to help ". Their first—and by no means last—contribution was £50,000. They added later further munificent sums, to open this door of sacred scholarship at Cambridge, in order that Methodist students may enter into the inheritance of its learning, and that, not as an end, but as a means of making them more efficient evangelists and pastors. We are thankful that this courageous friend and supreme benefactor of Wesley House lived long enough to see some of its sons leading in the saving of souls and the spreading of the Kingdom of God '.

The house at Brookside was obviously only a temporary home for our new enterprise at Cambridge. In October 1922 the House Committee of the Cambridge scheme bought a site from the authorities of Jesus College. It was situated in Jesus Lane, adjoining Jesus College, and was central to the life and work of the University. Plans were prepared by Sir Aston Webb, and on October 23, 1926, the College was opened amidst great rejoicing. Great difficulties had been overcome by the watchful care and devotion of Dr. Maldwyn Hughes. They had been made easier through the thoughtful co-operation of many friends of this new scheme in the University. At the opening of Wesley House—purposely called ' House ' and not 'College', so as to keep the University usage— the Vice-Chancellor of Cambridge University, the President of the Conference, and a most representative company of University and other friends of this new venture were present. The dedicatory sermon was preached by the President of the Conference (Rev. Dr. J. H. Ritson), his text being: ' Sir, we would see Jesus.' He said that ' Methodists throughout the world were full of gratitude to their friends in Cambridge, and especially to the authorities of Jesus College, for the kindly interest shown in this new foundation, and for the generous welcome extended to it. And Methodists, on their part, with the help of God, would ever seek to maintain the best traditions of that University, and to pursue its highest ideals. It was not criticism, but ignorance, that they feared in the realm of religion. They were there to seek knowledge that they might see Jesus. This House has been founded that men may so find Jesus that they may be able to go out into the world and show Him to all the human race '.

At the luncheon that followed the service, a speech was given by the Vice-Chancellor of the University (Dr. Seward), who offered his best wishes for the success of Wesley House. The next speaker was Rev. Dr. Nairne (Regius Professor of Divinity). We can still remember Dr. Nairne's heartfelt tribute to the hymns of the Wesleys—and his quoting, with such deep emotion:

Come, O thou traveller *unknown*.

He gave a most eager welcome to Wesley House. The Principal of Wesley House thanked the University for its cordial welcome given not only on this day, but ever since he came to Cambridge in 1921. He especially thanked the Master and Fellows of Jesus College, to whom they owed a great debt for the spirit in which the negotiations and other matters were carried out. He said: ' We have come to Cambridge primarily to breathe its atmosphere, and we venture to cherish the hope that we may make some slight contribution to the life of the University '. This hope has been certainly fulfilled, as is shown by the list of academic successes of

Wesley House men in the Tripos, and the winning of many University prizes by them. The last speaker was Mr. Gutteridge. It was in a true sense the crowning of his efforts, and was *his* day. It was a rare sight to see an old man of eighty-four, with his eyes beaming behind his spectacles, rejoicing in the accomplishment of a task which, at one time, seemed so impossible. Throughout that day the proceedings were permeated with a devout thankfulness that he had lived to see his dream come true. We remembered also those great helpers who had passed to the great beyond, but surely were with us in spirit, Mr. Greenhalgh, Mr. Ferens, Sir Henry Holloway, Mr. Albert E. Reed, and Mr. Williamson Lamplough.

Thus Wesley House came into being, through the vision of Mr. Michael Gutteridge and of Mr. William Greenhalgh, and by the help of its loyal friends and helpers —among whom we cannot refrain from mentioning Dr. J. H. Ritson, and Dr. W. T. A. Barber. The Report of 1927 refers to another noble gift to Wesley House : ' Mr. Edmund S. Lamplough has given to the trustees the sum of £5,000 for the erection of a Chapel in memory of the late Mr. Williamson Lamplough '. The final cost —defrayed in its entirety by Mr. Edmund S. Lamplough —was more than double that sum. The architect for this Chapel was Sir Aston Webb—who had planned the other buildings of Wesley House—and the work was accomplished by Mr. Maurice Webb. It was dedicated on May 17, 1930. It is panelled with English oak, and a tablet, suitably inscribed in Latin by Dr. Flew, records the devoted life and service of Mr. Williamson Lamplough. At the opening of the Chapel, Gipsy Smith, a great lover of Wesley House, was present. We mention his presence because it tells that Wesley House stands for Evangelism as well as learning. The Wesleyan Church and the University were well represented. Mr. Michael Gutteridge, owing to ill-health, could not be present—

but his son and grandson were there. The President of the Conference, Dr. W. F. Lofthouse, preached the dedicatory sermon, from the text : ' His glory . . . full of grace and truth ', and showed that in the service of religion there must be Beauty, Truth and Goodness. Since the opening, Mr. Harold Speed's beautiful fresco in the apse and the wall paintings have added more loveliness to this beautiful Chapel. ' The dominating figure is the glorified Christ, whose hands are out-stretched in blessing over the common activities of men, and over the beauty of the world. Herein we see the ideal for the life at Wesley House. The light in the picture is the light of the dawn. At the summit of the central archway is the Greek word for Hope, and the symbol beneath is of Him who is the Incarnate Hope of the storm-tossed world. The symbol is of victory, the Cross is in it, and it is a Cross borne by the Lamb of God.' The Chapel has become the centre of the life of Wesley House—morning and evening worship are held here daily—and rivers of rich influence have flowed from it into many lives. The Cambridge Group movement, which had its rise in Wesley House, has been greatly inspired by visions seen, and voices heard, in this Chapel.

Wesley House has now been in existence for fourteen years. It owes more than we can say to its two bene-factors Mr. Gutteridge and Mr. Greenhalgh. It also is much indebted to its Governors, who have given most freely of their love and service. We must mention the debt it owes to its first Principal, Dr. Maldwyn Hughes, who has been so greatly helped in the work at Wesley House by Mrs. Hughes. Dr. Hughes went to Cambridge with only a house as a temporary home for the new work. He has seen the buildings of Wesley House arise, and the work grow. He has built wisely and well. One of the first six students rightly speaks of ' the constant influence of Dr. Maldwyn Hughes, whose personality and strength were such that we loved him the more as months and years went on '. In 1928, an additional Tutor, Rev. R. Newton Flew (who was a little later to become the first Non-conformist by examination and thesis to obtain the Oxford B.D. and then the Oxford D.D.) was appointed. It was an admirable choice, and his coming to Wesley House brought to its help a scholar and an evangelist. Wesley House made the first practical experiment in Methodist Union—for before the Union of 1932, they had amongst their students accepted candidates of both the Primitive and United Methodist Churches. The work at Wesley House has been helped by an annual travelling scholarship, given by Mr. John Finch, of the value of £200. This scholarship has already been of great aid to certain Wesley House students and has enabled them to carry on research work at foreign Universities. Wesley House is an illustration of the fact that there is no opposition betwixt learning and evangelism. Many of its students are now on the high places of the field, and Tower Hill, Islington, Gateshead, Manchester, Edinburgh Missions, and our Circuits, tell of the evangelical fervour of its sons. Year by year the students of Wesley House take part in the Student Christian Movement missions in industrial towns. Both at home and abroad they are living witnesses of the words :

> 'Tis worth living for, this,
> To administer bliss
> And salvation in Jesus's name.

CHAPTER X

A GREAT CRUSADE

In 1925 Rev. Dr. John H. Ritson was elected President of the Conference. He was born at Bolton, went to Manchester Grammar School, and from there won a scholarship at Balliol College, Oxford, when Dr. Benjamin Jowett was the Master of that College. He entered the ministry in 1891, and has spent practically all his active ministerial life as one of the two Secretaries of the Bible Society. The brand, and it is a good one, is that of the three B's—Bolton, Balliol, Bible—and each strand is woven inextricably into the life of Dr. Ritson. In the year of his Presidency, Oxford gave to him *honoris causa* the degree of D.D. We remember that Degree Day, for we had the joy of being present.

A vision of God flashed before the eyes of Dr. Ritson, that vision made him see with vivid clearness that the training of its ministry is the most important task of the Church. He realized the need of the re-opening of Headingley, of a fuller equipment of our Colleges, of more adequate buildings, of extending the College course for a student to four years, and of the erection of College Chapels. There came to him the vision of a Church which should give to the training of its ministry a flaming enthusiasm, and a richer devotion and generosity. He realized that we had raised, in the last eighteen years, seven million pounds to erect churches, and rejoiced in this ; but he was profoundly convinced that the key position is that of the man who is in charge of the Church. He desired to awaken the Wesleyans to a new sense of responsibility, and to scatter the fires of this passion so that the whole Church should be aflame with his zeal.

A large vision flashed before the eyes of Dr. Ritson, and he determined that the Church should respond to its challenge. He desired to raise a quarter of a million pounds for the new claims of the Theological Colleges. He gained the permission of the Conference on behalf of this Crusade—but it must be clearly understood that his scheme was not a Connexional one. It had the imprimatur of the Conference upon it ; but it was not a Conference appeal in the name of the whole Church, such as were the Centenary and Thanksgiving Funds. There could be no general public appeal. The main driving force of this high emprise was prayer. It was begun, continued and ended in prayer ; and the goal was reached, for over £200,000 was raised in gifts ; and the new subscriptions when capitalized raised another £50,000, making a total of £250,000. It was a stupendous success, for the money was raised during years of severe commercial depression.

Dr. Ritson was splendidly supported in all his efforts by Mr. Edmund S. Lamplough (the Vice-President of the Conference for this year—1935). In 1926 Dr. Ritson became the ministerial Treasurer of the Theological Institution, and his colleague was Mr. T. S. Howorth, who for many years had done good service on behalf of that Fund. On Mr. Howorth's retirement from the post of Treasurer in 1927, his place was taken by Mr. Edmund Lamplough. The new effort on behalf of the Theological Institution was inaugurated when Dr. Ritson and Mr. Howorth were treasurers, and was brought to its successful conclusion by Dr. Ritson and Mr. Lamplough. Its chief aim was not financial, but to arouse a sense of the primary importance of the work of our Colleges ; to call the Church to prayer and to a deep sense of responsibility. A most important Conference was held at 'The Jordans ', where a group of devoted ministers and laymen of the Wesleyan Church gathered together from October 7 (Friday) to October 10 (Monday), 1927. The Conference

H

was addressed by Rev. Dr. Scott Lidgett, who spoke on
' The Training of the Ministry'; by Dr. C. Ryder Smith,
his subject being ' The Curriculum of Studies and the
Relation of our Colleges to the Universities '; by Rev.
T. H. Barratt, B.A., on ' Notes on Candidates for the
Wesleyan Ministry '; by Dr. W. T. A. Barber on ' The
Inner Life of the Colleges '; by Dr. A. W. Harrison on
' Notes on Reasons why Matriculation should be the
minimum standard for Candidates for the Ministry ';
by Dr. W. F. Lofthouse on ' The Present Training in our
Colleges '; and by Rev. C. W. Andrews on ' Spiritual
Training for the Ministry '. In many ways this Conference marked a new era. The central and immense
importance of the training of the ministry was the
dominant note of this most vital Conference. We will
give Dr. Scott Lidgett's words—spoken at ' The Jordans '
—for they focus and sum up these deliberations :

' The preparation and training of the ministry is the
greatest concern of Methodism at the present time. The
Church has, in recent years, carried through great
schemes of material expansion, in buildings. Educational
standards have risen throughout the country, and increased educational facilities of all kinds have been
multiplied. The educational requirements of every
profession, business and industry have become more and
more exacting. Yet the Wesleyan Methodist Church
has done little or nothing for more than forty years either
to raise the standard expected of Candidates for the
ministry or to improve their training when received.
The establishment of Wesley House, Cambridge, has
been the work of a handful of enlightened and generous
men, rather than of the Connexion as a whole. Yet the
supreme question is not that of church buildings, but of
the character, capacity, and equipment of the men who
minister in them.

' The highest concern of the Connexion, and the all-
embracing aim of the Colleges is spiritual and evangelical.

We need, above all, men of spiritual power to proclaim the Gospel, and so to present it as, by the blessing of God, to arouse, sustain and instruct the living faith that accepts it. Yet such faith is the act of a man's whole personality. The mind must co-operate with the heart and the will in its exercise. Hence, at the very least, the preacher must command the intellectual respect of his hearers, must be on a level with his congregation, and be in touch with their thought and difficulties, and particularly with those of the young. This requirement is made of the minister by all sections of society, not least of all by the most intelligent of the industrial classes.

' Furthermore, both the young minister and his hearers are confronted with problems of thought and life which go to the very heart of the Christian revelation and religion. When the minister as pastor comes into close and sympathetic contact with the young, he will be called upon not only to enter into their perplexities, but to give them such guidance as can only be furnished by one who has reached the level of intelligence, knowledge and outlook at which these perplexities chiefly arise. And this not as a merely intellectual end, but in order to win and maintain their allegiance to our Lord Jesus Christ. Hence the minister urgently needs, not indeed exact and expert scholarship, but reserves of thought and knowledge which can be mobilized and brought to bear upon his duties as both preacher and pastor.

' Yet even this vital necessity is secondary. What is even more important is the morale and virility of the minister. He must have grit, energy, and self-discipline if he is to discharge his task, and maintain his spiritual influence. The demand for these qualities must be made upon men at the outset. If a Candidate is to be received for training he should have satisfied the Church—his Ministers, his Circuit, and the Synod as well as the Connexional Authorities—that his sense of being called to the ministry has constrained him to fit himself to offer for it by availing himself of all the advantages and helps that are within his reach. This will give him the preliminary standard of education and knowledge which is needful, if his training in College is to have a hopeful start. If he fail to seek this he will come short not of a merely intellectual but of a moral, and in the last resort, a spiritual test that should be rigorously applied in order to discover his fitness for the highest of callings. The Ministers and Circuits who bring Candidates forward should be deeply impressed by this necessity, and should demand both that the prospective candidate should thoroughly prepare himself, and also give him all possible assistance in doing so. Should his disabilities or the lack of local facilities prevent him from obtaining this preliminary qualification, such co-operation between the Connexional and the Circuit Authorities should be established as will enable the candidate to reach the minimum standard before he is accepted for Ministerial Training. If the minimum standard for Candidates be raised, and if such steps be taken to enable those who fall short of it to reach it, not only will the general level of the ministry be raised and the work of the Colleges be made more effective, but a preliminary " discipline " will be applied, which will improve the morale of the Candidate and thus be of inestimable advantage to his character throughout the whole of his future ministry.

' If therefore, Methodism takes a sufficiently serious view of this gravely important subject, it will proceed without delay to take resolute steps to raise the standard required of candidates and to give them helpful guidance in attaining it. Then, having relieved the Colleges of elementary tasks which should not be thrown upon them, the Connexion should spare no pains and no outlay that are needed to make the Colleges and their training adequate to the searching and ever growing demands that are made of the Christian ministry in the present day.'

We have printed this address of Dr. Lidgett's at

length, because it sums up some of the main considerations of this Conference at ' The Jordans '.

Another theme of great importance discussed was that which was dealt with by Rev. T. H. Barratt. He had made a careful analysis of the occupations and education, prior to coming to College, of 424 students betwixt 1907 and 1927. He showed (1) the positions in life which they previously filled, (2) their intellectual equipment on entering College. This study showed clearly that the Wesleyan Church drew its Candidates far too much from one class, and also that, considering the great opportunities of Secondary Education, we obtained much too small a proportion of Candidates who had received a Secondary, and University education. It is of great importance to recall Mr. Barratt's main contention : ' The material from which the future ministry is to be made is a matter of as urgent importance as any question relating to the training that material may receive. As it is impossible to make bricks without straw, so it is impossible to turn out efficient evangelists, missionaries, and pastors from our Colleges, unless these Colleges are supplied with suitable material. The list of Candidates is the result of a combination of certain forces operating in the lives of the laity. It is often forgotten that the ministry is recruited exclusively from the laity'. In looking over the papers of this retreat, and this programme, we are struck by the thoroughness of the inquiry. All the stages of a young minister's life were considered—the days before candidature, the College training, the early years after leaving College, What, however, strikes us most of all is the way in which all discussion was interwoven with prayer, and that this ' Retreat ' tells of a dedication of a band of men to a great Crusade on behalf of a better and deeper training for the ministry—both intellectually and spiritually. The problem of finance was carefully reviewed by Rev. Thomas Kirkup, Mr. T. S. Howorth and Dr. J. H. Ritson ; but it was considered in the light of our great spiritual resources, and the victory was claimed by faith and prayer.

'The Jordans' conference was a House Beautiful from which those who had gathered there went forth to bring to a triumphal conclusion the task which God had entrusted to them. Meetings were held in various parts of the country—and a most generous response was made. When, in 1930, it was realized that it was financially possible, Headingley College, to the joy of its old students and of the Wesleyan Church in general, was reopened. As the Report for 1930-31 says: 'The opening of Headingley will not only relieve the pressure at the other Colleges, but will gladden the hearts of many who have longed to see the building used for its original purpose.'

About this time, a much needed and most welcome addition was made to our Colleges, for at each of them a College Chapel was built—at Didsbury it is called the 'Prayer Room'. The expense of building the Chapels at Richmond, Headingley and Handsworth was paid for by the money raised by the new Fund. Half the cost of the 'Prayer Room' at Didsbury was defrayed by Mr. Edmund S. Lamplough in memory of his brother, the late Mr. Williamson Lamplough, who for many years was Senior Treasurer of the Wesleyan Methodist Missionary Society, and a most valuable member of the Theological Institution Committee. This noble gift was, however, not included in the scope of the campaign, but was additional to it. It is impossible to tell the benefit of these Chapels in the life of the Colleges—the blessing which has come from them has been so immeasurably great. Before their erection, all devotional services, such as morning and evening Prayers, had been held in rooms which were used for many other purposes. Now we have the inestimable blessing of having a place of worship which is used only for worship. We speak what we know, when we say that this new addition to our Colleges has quickened the spiritual life of us all, by giving to us a place of quiet and prayer, where we meet for corporate worship, and where at all times of the day men can slip away from life's noise to the stillness and silence where we can say, ' this is none other than the house of God, and the very gate of heaven '. They have brought a new spirit of devotion to the Colleges.

In addition to the erection of Chapels at all the Colleges, most extensive alterations were made at Richmond. The new library there is, in our opinion, one of the most beautiful of all libraries. New class-rooms were built at Handsworth, and a most commodious common-room for the students ; new lecture-rooms were also built at Headingley, and a few alterations were made at Didsbury. Before these alterations, much of the work of the Colleges was, owing to lack of class-rooms, done under great difficulties. Now all our College buildings are thoroughly modernized, and the work can be done under the best conditions. All this is a great help.

Dr. Ritson in his clarion call to the members of the Wesleyan Church on behalf of the Colleges had appealed to those who could afford to do so, to ' Establish a Chair '. The amount of money needed to do this was £10,000. The ' Minutes of Conference ' reveals the fact that his appeal was responded to by the Hon. T. R. Ferens, Sir Thomas Rowbotham, Mr. Edmund S. Lamplough (at least on four occasions—for four ' Chairs ' were established by his generosity), the executors of Mr. R. H. Posnett, Mr. and the Hon. Mrs. J. Arthur Rank, Mr. George Shrubsall, Mr. and Mrs. H. W. Walker ; and Mr. Banks and Messrs. Crossfield together endowed one ' chair '. There are three endowed chairs at Didsbury College : the Lamplough Chair of Pastoral Theology and Church Organization, the Rowbotham Chair of English and the English Bible, the Robert H. Posnett Chair of New Testament Language and Literature ; there are three at Richmond : the Shrubsall Chair of Systematic

Theology, the Mr. and Mrs. H. W. Walker Chair of Philosophy, the Lamplough Chair of New Testament Language and Literature, and Classics; there are three at Headingley : the Lamplough Chair of Pastoral Theology, Church Organization and Hebrew; the Ferens Chair of New Testament Language and Literature, and Classics, the Banks-Crossfield Chair of Church History and History of Doctrine. At Hartley Victoria there are four : the A. S. Peake Chair of Old Testament Language and Literature, the Ranmoor Chair of Church History and English, the Duckworth Chair of New Testament Literature and Theology, the Lewins Chair of Philosophy. There are three at Handsworth : the Mr. and the Hon. Mrs. J. Arthur Rank Chair of Pastoral Theology, Church History and Organization, the Lamplough Chair of New Testament Language and Literature, and Classics, the Victoria Chair of Old Testament Language and Literature. At Wesley House, Cambridge, there are two : the Michael Gutteridge Chair of Systematic Theology, and the William Greenhalgh Chair of New Testament Language and Literature. There is a true fitness in there being four portraits of benefactors in the Dining Hall of Didsbury College, those of Sir Thomas Rowbotham, Mr. Robert H. Posnett, Mr. Edmund S. Lamplough, and Dr. J. H. Ritson. Dr. Ritson did not himself endow a ' chair ', but he inspired others to do so. Mr. Lamplough is there for two reasons—he gave a ' Chair ' at this College, and with Dr. Ritson was the great inspirer of these noble benefactions, and their names will always be associated in a special way not only with these gifts which tell of the endowment of ' Chairs ', but also because they inspired other gifts, many, but none the less generous, which were given by so many to this Fund to help forward the work of the training of the ministry. Dr. Ritson and Mr. Lamplough would disclaim any special praise and gratitude, and would point—and with good reason—to the advocacy of the leaders in the movement, and to the splendid help, both spiritual and financial, which was given by so many. The endowment of these ' Chairs ' not only relieves the annual financial problem, but also links with our Colleges the names of princely benefactors.

It had been the dream of many in the Wesleyan Church for a long time that the term of a student's residence at College should be lengthened, and that, when it was deemed to be desirable, students should be allowed to remain for four years in residence. Amongst the many blessings which Dr. Ritson's Crusade has brought to the Church, surely one of the greatest is that it seems probable that in the future an increasing number of students will be granted a fourth year. During the last two years a large number have had this benefit. So far this experiment has worked admirably, and we hope that it will not only continue—but continue on an extended scale.

Before the War, all our students, who were not graduates and desired to obtain a degree, became external Students of London University. Since the War great changes have taken place in this domain. Richmond is now a School of Divinity of London University. The relations between the Birmingham University and Handsworth are intimate, and there is close co-operation betwixt them. Didsbury is now in touch, through some of its students, with Manchester University. Headingley is not as yet able to co-operate with the Leeds University, because it has no Theological faculty. All the students of Wesley House are members of Cambridge University. Hartley College holds a pioneer place in this respect, and its life has for many years been closely woven with that of Manchester University. Before the Union of 1932 Victoria Park College, on the University side of its work, was in touch with London. But now the two Colleges have become one, Hartley Victoria is working in close co-operation with Manchester University.

Before Methodist Union came into being, Dr. Ritson

had been the inspiring genius of the re-opening of Headingley, of great material changes in our Colleges, and of
helping the Wesleyan Church to realize the central
importance of the training of its ministry. The movement he inaugurated became a spiritual crusade, and
brought blessing to staff, to students, and to our Church.
He brought to his task vision, large ideas, indefatigable
industry, a good generalship, and a mighty faith. He was
one of whom we can say :

> Languor is not in your heart,
> Weakness is not in your word,
> Weariness not on your brow.
> Ye alight in our van ! At your voice
> Panic, despair, flee away.

CHAPTER XI

HARTLEY PRIMITIVE METHODIST COLLEGE

By A. L. Humphries, M.A.

I

THE STORY OF THE BUILDING

It could be claimed that the story of Hartley College is virtually the history of ministerial education in the Primitive Methodist Church. Yet that qualified form of statement is necessary if certain movements in the direction of such education which preceded the opening of the College in 1881 are to receive the recognition they deserve. The Primitive Methodist Church emerged as a distinct religious organization in 1811, and for the first half-century of its existence it was content to dispense with any special training for its ministry. There are reasons which explain this. Primitive Methodism was born out of a passion for evangelism, and the first fifty years belong to the constructive and creative stage of its history. The eagerness to enter new openings and to break up ground previously untouched often led to men being thrust forth with very little warning or intellectual preparation to do the work of an evangelist. Financial difficulties also blocked the way, and there was the less effort to remove them because, apart from the apathy towards education, amounting almost to suspicion of it, which still remains one of the weaknesses of Englishmen, the work of Primitive Methodism during the last century lay almost entirely among working folk, who, having in those far-off days little education themselves, did not feel with any acuteness the lack of special education in their ministers. Nevertheless, some of the men who served the Primitive Methodist Church at that period of its history acquired, by dint of their own efforts, a creditable degree of culture. Such, to name but a few instances, were John Petty, Colin Campbell McKechnie, James Macpherson, and the brothers William and Samuel Antliff. What these men achieved for themselves they sought to stimulate in others. The establishment of the first Ministerial Association in 1850, issuing, as it did, a few years later in the founding of what, first known as *The Christian Ambassador*, functioned later and healthily as *The Holborn Review* (now combined with *The London Quarterly Review*), represented efforts to stimulate and guide the thinking of the more reflective of the ministers and laymen of the Church.

The help thus afforded to the ministry was, however, no adequate substitute for a preparatory training. The first impetus towards that came from the north. It was proposed at the Conference of 1865 that Elmfield College, York, which had been opened in the previous year as a Secondary School for boys, should be utilized also as a training centre for the ministry. The result was that from fifteen to twenty men were sent there in order to receive instruction for one year from the Rev. John Petty, a man at once scholarly and devout. In this way men like Thomas Mitchell and Edwin Dalton obtained some training prior to their entrance upon ministerial work. The next advance came three years later, when what became known as the Institute at Sunderland was opened, with Dr. William Antliff, then one of the most commanding figures in the life of the Church, as the first Principal and Tutor. The residence of students was for one year only, and the curriculum was a modest one, embracing certain features of ordinary education, as well as some attention to theology and subjects related to the work of preaching.

For the time being that step forward was thought sufficient. But in 1875 the desire for a College more central in its location and better adapted for its work

found expression. The original intention, however, was
not to displace the Institute at Sunderland, but to supplement it. Enthusiastic spirits, too, ventured to suggest
that the course of training ought to extend over two
years—a dream, however, which had to wait nearly
seventeen years before it was realized. The decision was
ultimately reached that a second College or Institute
should be established, and that its location should be
Manchester. That choice was dictated partly by the fact
that Manchester, as regards the country at large, was
fairly central in situation, and it was moreover, as regards
Primitive Methodism, in close proximity to quite a
number of vigorous Circuits, in which students belonging
to a College in Manchester would have those frequent
opportunities for preaching which were felt to be desirable
as part of their training. But there was another important factor in the choice. Owens College did not then
possess the prestige which now attaches to it as ' The
Victoria University of Manchester ', but even then it was
doing excellent work, and was specially dear to Free
Churchmen because of its broad and unsectarian spirit.
It was seen that ministerial students belonging to a College
founded in its neighbourhood might be able to attend
some of its classes, and thus acquire an even wider
training than their own Church could provide. This
hope was realized in a number of cases. Much more than
that, however, ultimately came to pass. The elevation of
Owens College to University rank, and the establishment
within it in due course of a Theological Faculty, with a
member of the teaching staff of Hartley College, Dr.
Peake, as the first Rylands Professor of Biblical Exegesis
and Dean of the Faculty, and the consequent training
within the University of a considerable number of Hartley
students, who, having matriculated, were free to take the
Arts and Divinity Courses—these were developments
which were not seen even on the far horizon by those men
who sought to found the new College for Primitive

Methodism at Manchester.   Surely the men of 1875, like all who move under the guidance of Divine Providence, ' builded wiser than they knew '.

Two of the active spirits in the new enterprise were James Travis and William Beckworth, the former a minister sagacious in judgement and energetic in action, highly esteemed not only in Lancashire but all over the Primitive Methodist Church ; the latter a layman, cultured in mind and eloquent of tongue, and occupying a prominent place in the civic and religious life of Leeds. Mr. Travis did yeoman service in raising funds for the new scheme.   He was then steadily climbing to that great Connexional reputation which he subsequently gained and bore with so much distinction.   How much he did for the College in those preliminary years it would be difficult to say.   Men trusted his judgement and felt the spell of his forceful and persuasive speech.   Thanks largely to his efforts the Conference of 1876 could be told that already £2,000 had been promised, and the new scheme went forward with Conferential approval, though with the proviso that the erection of a building—the site had already been secured—should not be undertaken until sufficient further financial support was forthcoming to warrant the hope that the College would be opened free of debt.   The wise condition necessitated two years' delay. It was not until June 24, 1878, that the Memorial Stone-laying took place.   The Conference was then in session in Manchester, and the Stonelaying in connexion with the new College was one of the outstanding events in its proceedings.   The present writer, who was then a boy in Liverpool, has but one memory of that Conference. He can remember that his father, coming one day as a visitor to the Conference and listening to the discussions, told him on his return that it had been decided ' to break down the barriers '.   By some people that decision was regarded as almost equivalent to revolution.   To remove the restrictions by which ministers had previously been

compelled to ' travel ' within the limits of a particular
District, and to give them liberty to accept an invitation
from any District and Circuit, was a large and far-reaching
policy. But surely the foundation of the College was,
in the light of subsequent history, a much more significant
removal of barriers. Doubtless it was wise to enlarge
the sphere of those who were already in the ministry, but
how much more necessary it was to give to those who
stood upon its threshold some training in the theme and
methods of their vocation, without which even the man
called of God must in these modern days feel diffident
and bound !

It is interesting to recall that the contractor who undertook the erection of the building which served as the
original College was Mr. J. Gerrard, the father of the
present Treasurer of Hartley College. His estimate
for the erection was nearly £5,700. This estimate,
however, did not include architect's fees, cost of furnishing, and other important expenditure, and hence the total
outlay amounted finally to £8,200. Still it did not seem
an idle hope that the building might be opened free of
debt, seeing that the amount actually paid or promised at
the time of the Stonelaying was £5,345. Upon the
Rev. James Macpherson devolved the work of securing
further financial assistance. He had already been desig-
nated as Principal and Tutor of the new institution, but
for the time being he had to serve as Secretary and Financial Agent. His task was not an easy one. The country
had passed into the trough of a serious commercial
depression, and the time was not auspicious for the raising
of money. Not only was the inflow of fresh promises
checked, but in a number of cases the fulfilment of
promises already made became impossible. The result
was that the Conference of 1881 found the building
complete, but encumbered with a debt of £1,670. In
spite of this fact the Conference was asked to permit the
College to be opened, and to this request it, in view of all

the circumstances, acceded. Accordingly, towards the end of July, 1881, the first company of students, ten in number, was admitted. The number admitted was small —much smaller than the total accommodation, which was for thirty, would have permitted—but it has to be borne in mind that the opening of this new institution at Manchester had not meant the closing down of the one already existing at Sunderland. The two institutions were for the moment pursuing their work side by side, with the unforeseen result that, at the following Conference, difficulty was found in providing stations for all the men who had completed their course of training. The supply was in excess of the demand, and it was felt advisable to close both the Colleges for a year. In the case of the one at Sunderland this step proved to be the end of its useful career. Seeing that the building at Manchester was more modern and had larger accommodation, it was decided to concentrate the work of ministerial training there, and to dispose of the older institution. That course was ultimately followed, and the proceeds of the sale were applied to the reduction of the debt at Manchester. Unfortunately the spectre of financial anxiety haunted the College through all the early years of its history. Quite apart from the burden of debt lingering on the building, the account for working expenses was invariably overdrawn.

The main source of income was the students' fees. These, for the one year of residence, were £30 each, though a reduction was occasionally made in the case of those students who could not conveniently pay the full amount. It often happened, however, that the College Committee, because of its own straitened circumstances, could not grant remissions where otherwise it would have been glad to concede them. The Conference Fund, as the general working Fund at the disposal of the Conference was then called, was unable to make to the College more than limited and insufficient grants. All this meant that

HARTLEY VICTORIA COLLEGE, MANCHESTER.

the Committee had to depend to a considerable extent on the precarious income derived from public collections and from the donations of sympathizers. Too much praise cannot be given to the men who, during those difficult and anxious years, managed the affairs of the College and kept it going. The Church had called it into being, but it was unprepared as yet to make the financial sacrifices which were necessary for its efficient maintenance. Melancholy evidence of this was afforded by the replies which the various Districts in 1887 sent in response to a circular inquiring whether they approved of the expenses of the College being met by an annual levy of one half-penny per member. Sad to relate, only three Districts approved of the suggestion; the rest were in favour of letting matters drift on as they were. Doubtless some excuse for this attitude could be found in the pressure of local claims. The basic fact, however, was that the College, during this initial period of its existence, had not captured the imagination of Primitive Methodists, and hence there was no earnest and widespread disposition to support an institution the serious need for which was not sufficiently realized.

The longest lane, however, has a turning, and a happier day dawned when, in 1888, the last portion of the building debt was removed. In due course, too—though not till several years after that date—the reorganization of Church's finances and the establishment by a system of levy on the circuits of what became familiarly known as 'The Connexion Fund', enabled the financial needs of the College to be met each year by a grant from that Fund, and appeals to Circuits for special collections became, happily, a thing of the past. There were other changes, too, of which we need to tell. In 1889 Mr. Macpherson felt compelled, by reason of age, to retire from the office of Principal. His successor was the Rev. Dr. Joseph Wood. Mr. Macpherson, however, still continued to render tutorial assistance, and it was not

I

until three years later that his service to the College finally ceased. His portrait, as also that of the Rev. James Travis, hangs on the walls of the College library as a permanent memorial of his connexion with the College and his valuable services to it. His successor was a man of a different type. Alert in mind and often pungent in speech, Dr. Wood brought with him the gift of new ideas. Throughout his term of office—he retired in 1893 —he strove to popularize the College and to put its affairs on a more satisfactory basis. The most notable event associated with his Principalship was the accession to the College of Mr. A. S. Peake. Dr. Peake, to use what afterwards became his familiar designation, was the son of a Primitive Methodist minister, and was himself a local preacher. After a distinguished career at Oxford, the crowning achievement of which was his election as a Fellow of Merton College, he had been appointed a lecturer at Mansfield College, then under the rule of Dr. Fairbairn. It was at this stage in Dr. Peake's career that Sir W. P. Hartley (to use for him also his later designation), who happened to be on a visit to Oxford, made his acquaintance, the medium of their introduction to each other being the Rev. J. Harryman Taylor, who was at the time a student at Mansfield College in preparation for the Primitive Methodist ministry. Sir William became impressed with the importance of securing Dr. Peake's services for the College at Manchester. For the latter to leave Oxford was no light sacrifice, but when he was approached with a definite invitation to come to Manchester, his strong sense of duty, confirmed, as it was, by the judgement of Dr. Fairbairn, induced him to consent. It was a happy and momentous decision. The financial difficulties which hedged this new departure were removed by Sir William Hartley's generous offer to defray, for a period of five years, the extra expenditure involved, his stipulation, however, being that the course of training at the College should be lengthened to two years. The

Conference of 1892, with great readiness, confirmed these arrangements, and in the July of that year Dr. Peake entered upon his duties. What his presence on the teaching staff of the College meant as regards the curriculum must be told later. It is sufficient at the moment to say that from that date until his death thirty-seven years later, Dr. Peake, as much by the fine quality of his personality as by the wonderful range of his learning, held under his magic spell the successive generations of students who sat at his feet, and laid them and the whole Church under a debt the measure of which can never be fully assessed.

Dr. Peake's coming led to changes in more than the nature and range of the teaching. With a two years' course of training prescribed, and yet with accommodation for only thirty students, the College could not supply more than fifteen men each year for the needs of Circuits. This number was inadequate, and hence the enlargement of the College soon became imperative. The problem was carefully considered by the Committee, land secured, plans prepared, and even an estimate of the cost obtained. This was the situation when the Conference met at Edinburgh in the year 1895. The Church was then in the midst of its efforts to raise the Jubilee Thanksgiving Fund, one-fourth of the proceeds of which were to be devoted to the College. It seemed likely that the greater part of the money which the College was thus due to receive would be absorbed by the proposed extension of the buildings, and that little or nothing would be left for other purposes. Sir William Hartley was anxious, however, that the course of training should ultimately be extended to three years, and that there should be a source from which financial help might be rendered to students who, because of straitened circumstances, found difficulty in meeting their College expenses. These generous desires, so characteristic of the man, led him to come forward at Edinburgh and offer to defray the entire cost of the enlargement, subject to the College allocation from the Jubilee Fund being left unaffected and being available for the purposes named. The Conference gratefully accepted the offer. The extension involved the duplication of the existing study-block, the provision of a new dining-hall, a lecture-room, and a common-room, the tower with its clock, and other items of value. Its formal dedication was the outstanding feature of the Conference of 1897. That Conference did more than accept the gift and honour the giver. It gave the College the full complement of sixty students for which it now had accommodation. The hope indulged was that, with the numbers maintained year by year at this level, it would be possible to meet the requirements of stationing, and yet permit students who desired it to remain for a third year of training. This hope was largely disappointed. The demands of stationing proved greater than had been anticipated, with the result that it sometimes happened that even the thirty men with two years' training which the College could supply proved insufficient. This involved that men who had passed the Candidates' Examination and who were in many cases anxious to enter the College, were sent direct into the ministry. This unsatisfactory procedure was alleviated by temporary accommodation being provided for an additional twelve students in 1902. Even then, however, only a small minority of the students had the opportunity of remaining at College for more than two years. Under these circumstances Sir William Hartley, being anxious that three years should become for every man the normal College course, offered at the Conference of 1903 to defray the cost of another enlargement of the College, subject to the Church becoming responsible for its due maintenance when complete. That offer saw visible fulfilment at the Conference of 1906, which, like those of 1878 and 1897, was held in Manchester. The formal dedication of this second enlargement was a great occasion. A service was held in the College chapel with Dr. Fairbairn as the preacher. A short meeting in a tent in the grounds followed, and the proceedings culminated in a great demonstration in the Free Trade Hall, with Sir William Hartley in the chair. The meeting was remarkable for the tribute which the audience paid to the chairman and Dr. Peake, one, the far-sighted layman who had made so generous a gift, the other, the scholar, the value of whose work had made the gift so desirable. It was also an extremely happy circumstance that Mr. Travis and Mr. Beckworth, who had played so large a part in securing the erection of the first building, were able to take an honoured part in the day's proceedings, and to see in this final enlargement of the College more than the fulfilment of all their dreams.

Something needs to be said as to the nature of this final extension. To describe it in detail in impossible. It involved, to begin with, the acquisition of additional land. The site now in possession of the College covers more than five and a half acres. As regards the main building, the chief items in the 1906 extension were the study-block and the chapel. The former consists, on three of its sides, of studies. These, as regards the corridor on to which they open, were so arranged that no study faces north. Each room, therefore, obtains during some part of the day a share of such sunshine as Manchester skies permit its inhabitants to receive. The front of the study-block consists on the ground floor of rooms for the Tutors and Committee, and on the floor above of sick rooms, where any dangerous case of illness can be isolated. Across the corridor from the Tutors' rooms is the large lecture-room, lighted from the back, and capable of accommodating the whole of the students, whose desks are arranged on a rising gallery so that lecturer and students have a clear view of each other. The study-block contains nearly one hundred and thirty rooms. Beyond this section of the College is the chapel. This was not in the scheme of extension as it was planned in the first instance, but Sir William Hartley readily consented to include it when a persuasive pressure was laid upon him to do so. The chapel is beautiful in its simplicity. It is substantially built and has sitting accommodation for 160 persons. The woodwork is all of selected oak, slightly wax-polished.

The 1906 enlargement included some important additions to that portion of the College, also Sir William Hartley's gift, which was opened in 1897. What had previously been the dining-hall was converted into a lecture-room, and a new dining-hall was erected, conveniently adjacent to the kitchens and double the size of the old one. Moreover, what had previously served as both common-room and library had its roof lifted and a storey added, the original room becoming a common-room, whilst the new room above it was set apart as a library. This was another addition to the original plans. The library is a light, airy room, specially fitted with dust-proof bookcases. On its walls there hang portraits of Sir William Hartley, Dr. Peake, James Travis, and other connexional worthies, the memory of whose work the College desires to preserve. The effect of the final enlargement, which we have described, was to put the College in possession of a building, commodious in its accommodation and admirably adapted for the purposes it had to serve. The land and building must represent, even in pre-war values, nearly £50,000. The greater part of this was the gift of Sir William Hartley. What his noble benefaction meant in time and thought, as well as money, can never be told. It involved the gift of himself as well as of his substance. It was a small but fitting recognition of the debt which ministerial education in the Primitive Methodist Church owed to him that since 1906 the College, by special resolution of the Conference, has borne his name, and is familiarly known and described as ' Hartley College '.

2

THE INNER LIFE OF THE COLLEGE

JUST as there was development in the building, so was there progress in the curriculum. It is interesting to look back now upon the course of study which the students in the 'eighties pursued. Theology was studied with Pope's learned work on it as the text-book. Angus' *Bible Handbook* was also in use. Other subjects and text-books were Waylands' *Moral Science*, Jevons' *Logic*, Whateley's *Rhetoric*, and Phelps' *Homiletics*. Added to these were elementary subjects such as Geography, Arithmetic, Grammar, and English History, whilst some attention was also devoted to the History of Primitive Methodism and to Church History in general. In point of quantity, therefore, the course covered a great deal of ground, and it is scarcely matter for wonder that more than once it was found impossible to traverse the whole of it within the compass of a single year. It is on its quality that it seems most open to criticism. On the Biblical and Theological side it exhibited some serious omissions. No attempt seems to have been made to take the students to the Bible itself and to unfold its history and significance. 'The Bible,' says one of the students of those early days, 'was the one text-book we never required in class, and it was not used except as a book of reference.' No attempt, either, was made to give the students instruction in Hebrew or Greek. Yet we would not be understood as casting any reflection upon Mr. Macpherson by these criticisms. The curriculum was not wholly of his ordaining. If he had had his way, it would have been of a more advanced character, and some of the elementary subjects, the study of which to a portion at least of the students was a sheer waste of time, would have been displaced. But he was not free to do just as he pleased. There was prejudice to be encountered in the Church, and among ministers as well as laymen, and this had its influence in the regulation of the course of studies.

Moreover, what are we to think of the amazing arrangement by which one man was expected to teach all the subjects embraced in the curriculum, as well as administer the affairs of the institution ? Under such conditions no teacher, let him be ever so capable, could make his teaching equally efficient throughout. What happened was that a number of the subjects, such as Theology, Logic, and Moral Science, were regularly dealt with in class, but, in the case of others, the student had to trust to his private reading, supplemented by occasional treatment of them in the class-room. Nevertheless, the training given was not without its value. Apart from the useful information which men obtained, they acquired regular habits of study, and derived mental and moral stimulus from their fellowship with each other. Mr. Macpherson's strong intellectual qualities also left their mark. One of his old students says of him : ' He was a modern Titan, a man of large proportions of stature and mind. He was scholarly, industrious, with a genius for taking pains. He lacked the softer and more human side of an ideal tutor, but one could not but admire his even habits, as of a machine, the mark of thoroughness in all he did, the freedom from the smaller caprices and feelings of human nature, and his quick sympathy with any one who showed intellectual fitness or desire '. He did a good day's work in a difficult time, and his name deserves an honourable place in this record.

A new era opened when, in 1892, Dr. Peake was appointed Tutor. He was deeply impressed with the vital importance of securing for the ministry as thorough a familiarity with Scripture in the light of the best modern knowledge as was possible to students in their brief time of residence. With this object in view he introduced at once into the curriculum six distinct Biblical courses, three of which dealt with the Old Testament and three with the New. The general idea underlying the Biblical work was that a comprehensive study of the subject should be combined with close, detailed study of special portions. Thus the courses in Old and New Testament Introduction carried the students over the problems of date, authorship, and literary structure of the books of the Bible. In the Old Testament the course included the Pentateuch, the Historical books, and the Poetical and Wisdom literature ; in the New Testament, the Gospels, the Acts, and the Pauline Epistles. The courses in Old and New Testament Theology sought to exhibit the growth of the religion of Israel and primitive Christianity. They embraced a sketch of the history of the Hebrew religion, with special reference to the Semitic basis and to the growth of religious institutions, a more detailed exposition of the teaching of the prophets, and full treatment of the Pauline Theology, and the teaching of Hebrews, 1 Peter, and the Apocalypse. All these courses may be described as general in scope and character. The courses in Biblical Exegesis were intended to supplement these by a more minute and special study of the text. In the Old Testament Isaiah i–xxxix was generally taken, though other portions were occasionally included. In the New Testament, Romans and Colossians were the books on which Dr. Peake lectured, while New Testament Exegesis remained one of his subjects. Systematic, as well as Pastoral, Theology remained in the hands of the Principal, Dr. Wood. In order, however, to supply not simply a Biblical but an historical basis for the former, Dr. Peake for a number of years gave a course of lectures on the History of Doctrine, his survey being confined to the first few centuries of the Christian era.

The changes which Dr. Peake thus initiated amounted to a revolution in the curriculum of the College. Yet it was a revolution which was opportune and necessary.

Apart from the defects which, quite unavoidably, belonged to the previous curriculum, religious thought concerning the Bible was at the time of Dr. Peake's advent to the College in a state of flux. Wellhausen had spoken in Germany and Robertson Smith in our own country. Nor were these the only voices which challenged the traditional view of the Bible. Doubt is always paralysing, and the Christian ministry least of all could afford to be in uncertainty as to the Divine authority and inspiration of the Scriptures. It was singularly fortunate, therefore, that there was enlisted in the service of the College, in the person of Dr. Peake, a man supremely competent to mediate the new truth concerning the Bible to the minds of the rising ministry, and yet always careful and even eager so to present it that those who heard him felt that everything which mattered in the traditional faith was not only preserved, but confirmed and enriched. Dr. Peake's teaching was never merely negative and destructive. In the end, as all his students would testify, it made for a surer and richer faith. Hence those who sat at his feet, while constantly amazed at the wealth of his learning, honoured and loved him. Nor was teaching the only way in which he served the interests of the College. He took part in the wider life of the Church, preaching in her pulpits and speaking on her platforms, and always commending himself as well as his message by the spirit and grace of his utterance. Men recognized in his speech the authentic evangelical note. They felt that he was not only a great scholar, but a devout and convinced Christian. The charm of his personality and his simple goodness allayed fears and disarmed suspicion. Men came to believe in his work because they were led to believe in him. In several of the tributes which were paid to him at the time of his death it was pointed out, as his crowning achievement, that in a Church inclined by tradition to be conservative in its point of view, he had successfully conducted its ministry and its thoughtful laymen over from the old conception of the Bible to the new, without any of the acute and bitter controversies which might have attended that transition. That achievement was due to the character of the man as well as to the quality of his teaching.

The College grew in popular favour, and the Primitive Methodist Church became ready to follow the lead of Sir William Hartley in all the developments which his munificence made possible. In other ways Dr. Peake's worth came to be recognized and his services utilized. The Lancashire Independent College added him to its staff; he served also for a time the United Methodist College; Manchester University, as already narrated, appointed him as its first Rylands Professor of Biblical Exegesis; the National Evangelical Free Church Council honoured itself as well as him by electing him as its President; The Universities of Aberdeen and Oxford, the latter his *alma mater*, recognized his scholarship and his contributions to religious literature by conferring upon him the Hon. D.D. degree. Last, but not least worthy to be named, his was one of the most potent voices, especially when negotiations were at a critical stage, in shaping the judgement of the Methodist Union Committee and in commending the policy of Union to the approval of his Church. He was not spared to see the achievement of that for which he wrought with such ability and force. Take him all in all, Dr. Peake was one of the greatest gifts God has ever bestowed upon Hartley College in the first instance, for there lay his supreme work, and then upon the whole Church to which he belonged. We thank God upon every remembrance of him.

We return to our survey of the curriculum and its changes. For a year after his coming to the College Dr. Peake included New Testament Greek in the subjects which he taught. In the following year, however, the Rev. D. Neilson, M.A., B.D., was engaged as an Assistant Tutor for the teaching of this subject, and he discharged this duty with energy and enthusiasm and to the great benefit of the students committed to his care while his connexion with the College lasted. In 1893 the Rev. John Watson succeeded Dr. Wood in the Principalship. He retained the subjects taught by his predecessor, but, as time and opportunity offered, added Logic and Psychology to his course. He also introduced German as an optional subject. The completion of the first enlargement of the College in 1897 was the occasion of the admission of a large number of new students. Notwithstanding this the staff was not increased, the Committee having in mind the fact that there were no third-year students, and that Dr. Watson's term as Principal was due to expire in the following year. A special Committee was appointed to consider how best to carry forward the work of the College when the change of Principal took place. It was decided to recommend that Dr. Watson's connexion with the College should be continued. This suggestion the Conference of 1898 accepted. Dr. Watson was appointed to a Manchester Circuit, with an assistant, and remained a Tutor of the College. The staff then consisted of the new Principal, the Rev. G. Parkin, M.A., B.D., and Dr. Peake, with Mr. Neilson and Dr. Watson, both with the responsibility of circuits, as Assistant Tutors. Up to this time Systematic Theology had always been taught by the Principal. Since, however, Dr. Watson had been teaching this subject for the previous five years, it was agreed, with the hearty concurrence of the new Principal, that he should continue to teach this as well as certain other subjects which had previously belonged to him. Mr. Parkin's accession to the staff made a great advance possible, for in addition to teaching Pastoral Theology and Homiletics, which were subjects naturally falling to him as Principal, he commenced classes in Hebrew, which has ever since remained an integral part of the curriculum of the College. In addition to this he lectured on New Testament Exegesis, which was relinquished to him by Dr. Peake at his special request.

This situation remained unchanged for several years. However, in September 1901, Dr. Watson was struck down by a serious illness, which made continuance of his work at the College impossible. For the remainder of the Connexional year his colleagues did their best to supply his place; but it was obvious that a new step would have to be taken by the substitution for the two Assistant Tutors of a Tutor with complete freedom from Circuit responsibilities. The result was that the Conference of 1902 appointed the Rev. A. L. Humphries, M.A., as second Tutor. He took over the subjects which had been taught by Mr. Neilson and Dr. Watson, except that, by arrangement with the Principal, there was an exchange between them of Systematic Theology and New Testament Exegesis. This arrangement also continued during the term of the succeeding Principal, the Rev. W. Johnson. From 1908, however, Mr. Humphries undertook the teaching of Systematic Theology, and that subject, with New Testament Greek, has remained ever since his chief share of the curriculum of the College. In lectures spread over three years he has dealt successively with ' The Doctrine of Sin ', ' The Person of Christ ', and ' The Doctrine of the Atonement ', those three themes being regarded by him as lying at the very heart of the evangelical faith. After Dr. Peake's death he also took over that part of Dr. Peake's work which was concerned with the Synoptic Problem and Teaching, and he gave, too, some lectures, as Dr. Peake did, of a preparatory nature on the problems of Inspiration and Revelation. In 1903 Dr. Wardle was added to the College staff. This was done on the initiative and, at first, at the expense of Sir W. P. Hartley, who was anxious that the students should have a more thorough grounding in English both by means of lectures and by criticism of essays, which it became part of their work to supply. The teaching of Hebrew also ceased to be the work of the Principal and was assigned to Dr. Wardle. No further change took place till 1908. In that year Mr. Atkinson Lee, M.A., who was serving the University of Wales as a Lecturer at Aberystwyth, was invited to join the teaching staff of the College. The desire underlying the invitation was to strengthen the curriculum on the Moral Science side, especially as the presence of students staying for a third year had made urgent the addition to the staff of an expert in Philosophy. Professor Lee took over from Professor Humphries the teaching of Logic and Psychology, and he also ultimately expanded his own treatment of Metaphysics so as to make it include the Philosophy of Religion. The staff now consisted of a Principal and four Tutors—sufficient at length to compass the various phases of the training which it was felt necessary to give to the future ministry of the Primitive Methodist Church, and except that according to the usage of that Church a new Principal assumed the reins of office at the end of every five years, there was no change in its personnel till the death of Dr. Peake.

In 1913 Dr. Peake completed twenty-one years in the service of the College. The Committee, acting on the suggestion of its Secretary, the Rev. G. Armitage, decided that this event called for special recognition. Plans were made to this end, but it was not until June of the following year that they came to fruition. The recognition of Dr. Peake's services took several forms. One was the enrichment of the College Chapel by the insertion of three stained-glass windows. They were designed by Mr. Anning Bell, and were the personal gift of Sir William Hartley.

A bronze tablet underneath the central window speaks of Dr. Peake's ' distinguished service ' as a Tutor of the College, and ' his valuable contribution to Biblical scholarship ', which the three windows were intended to commemorate. Old students of Dr. Peake and admirers scattered all over our Church combined by their gifts to provide other tokens of appreciation. His portrait in academic robes, painted by Mr. A. T. Nowell, was unveiled by the Rev. John Day Thompson ; it now hangs in the College library. At the tea, which followed the proceedings in the Chapel, speeches, warm in the praise of Dr. Peake and his work, were delivered by Professor F. E. Weiss, the Vice-Chancellor of the University, Dr. James Hope Moulton, Professor Humphries, and others, whilst Mr. T. L. Gerrard, the College Treasurer, made a presentation of silver to Dr. and Mrs. Peake. What to Dr. Peake greatly enhanced the pleasure which this celebration gave him was that it was made the occasion of the founding of a number of scholarships and half-scholarships for needy students.

The Great War, as might be expected, wrought havoc with the work of the College. It not only checked the inflow of fresh students ; it led to the exodus of some who were already resident at the College. On a memorable occasion nearly thirty of the latter marched to the Manchester Town Hall that they might offer their services to the R.A.M.C. We sorrow to relate that two who thus saw service abroad were not permitted to return. In June 1917, it was decided to close the College, and for the next two years that portion of the buildings representing the first and second extensions was taken over by the Red Cross Society and utilized as a military hospital. It proved well adapted for this purpose, and over 2,000 cases of suffering were dealt with whilst this arrangement was in force. In March 1919, classes for some students —seventeen in number—who had been demobilized, were instituted in the old wing of the College, and to that partial extent the work of ministerial training was resumed.

It was not, however, till August 1919, that the College buildings reverted to their ordinary use and tutors and students resumed their old duties. But it was with one important difference. The United Methodist

College in Victoria Park was left at the moment with but one person on its staff, the then Principal, the Rev. J. T. Brewis, B.A., B.D. As a friendly act it was arranged that the Hartley staff and Principal Brewis should co-operate for that year in the training of the men belonging to the two Colleges. This arrangement proved so mutually satisfactory that though Mr. Brewis was joined in 1920 by two colleagues, the Rev. G. G. Hornby, M.A., B.D., and Rev. E. W. Hirst, M.A., B.Sc., that co-operative action was continued with great advantage to both Colleges, so that it became a happy and settled practice. No one in either of the two Churches ever thought of disturbing it. It enabled new subjects, of great value, to be added to the curriculum and others already there to be taught more efficiently. The co-operation of the two tutorial staffs proved of inestimable service in the critical situation caused by the death of Dr. Peake. That grievous loss befell the College in August, 1929. What it meant for that great scholar and teacher, who had filled so large a place in the life of the College, to be with such little warning taken away, can be more easily imagined than described. The College year was just on the point of commencing, and yet no appointment to fill the vacancy could be made until the following June. Happily the co-operation of the United Methodist staff with that of Hartley eased the situation, and made temporary arrangements for doing much of what had been Dr. Peake's work possible. Moreover, advantage was taken of the interval represented by the vacancy to review with care the whole work of the curriculum, with a view to its more satisfactory distribution among the two tutorial staffs, and to deciding what work a new Tutor, if appointed, should be required to do. The scheme of re-distribution which was devised and, when submitted to the Conference, was ultimately approved, was greatly facilitated by the working arrangement between the two Colleges. It may be added that the Rev. H. G. Meecham,

M.A., Ph.D., was in due course elected to fill the vacancy on the Hartley College staff.

This record would be sadly incomplete if it failed to make honourable mention of a number of names which, by virtue of the worth and service of those to whom they belong, deserve a place in this story. To begin with, what a fine succession of Principals the College has had at its head during the last fifty years! Extended reference has already been made to the earliest of them—James Macpherson, Joseph Wood, and John Watson—but they were followed by William Johnson, W. Jones-Davies, Henry J. Pickett and James Lockhart. ' All these were honoured in their generations, and were a glory in their days.' The names recall variety of type and diversity of aptitudes, but the men who bore them did yeoman service to the College, not less by the quality of their personality than by the nature of their gifts, and they are rightly held in honour. Of those named, Mr. Pickett had the unique distinction of having been appointed to the Principalship for a second term. The present holder of the office, Dr. Wardle, stands in worthy succession to those who have preceded him. The College has been most fortunate in its Treasurers. The first one was Mr. John Lees Buckley, of Woodley. He died, however, whilst the first building was in process of erection, and his son, Mr. Samuel Buckley, succeeded to the office. When he resigned in 1887, Ald. Thomas Beeley, J.P., was appointed. He held the office until his death twenty years later, and was succeeded by his son, Mr. T. Carter Beeley, whose tenure of it—all too brief, as it proved, for it only lasted twelve months—was also terminated by death. For nearly thirty years now the Treasurer has been Ald. T. L. Gerrard, J.P., of Swinton, whose efficient oversight of the finances of the Colleges and constant interest in all that pertains to its welfare have won for him the affectionate esteem of all who have had the privilege of knowing him and his work.

K

As we close this chronicle we are conscious of its in-completeness. As regards the curriculum, *e.g.*, nothing has been said about the lectures, provided in part from without, on Child Psychology and Sunday School Organization, and the instruction of the students in Elocution and Voice-production—two things which have long been an integral part of the course of training. Nor would we leave unmentioned the keen interest which the students have always shown in Foreign Missions. The flame of missionary enthusiasm burns high in the College. There has never been any lack of volunteers for the foreign field, and the Missionary Anniversary and the College Garden Party—twin efforts which, in the aggre-gate, must have raised thousands of pounds for missions —have become established features of the College year. The inner life of the College, too, has been kept healthy. The devotional services in the College chapel, group-fellowships for the more intensive study of the problems of religious life and social duty, the cultivation of the spirit of prayer, have all made for the hallowing of thought and life. A large company of men in the ministry to-day look back with gratitude upon all that the College did for them. Hartley College, thanks to great souls who have loved and served it, has had a wonderful past. Whilst alive to the modern spirit and clear-eyed to all new expressions of truth, it has kept faithful to the evangelical tradition. And when, by the consummation of Methodist Union, Primitive Method-ism became merged in a larger fellowship, Hartley College, in virtue of what it had been and is, was not unworthy to take its place by the side of the other Colleges which now form the Theological Institution of the one Methodist Church.

A few recent happenings must be mentioned if this record is to be up to date. The fusion of what were three Methodist Churches into one has meant change as regards the Theological Colleges of Methodism. It was felt that there needed to be some reduction in their number, especially in Manchester, where Methodism rejoiced in the existence of three Colleges. In 1934 the Committee of the Victoria Park College, this being the smallest of the three, offered with great magnanimity to close down that College and to transfer its students and staff and funds. The students and staff passed over to Hartley College, with which the Victoria Park College had had such long and happy co-operation. The friendship between the two Colleges found expression also in the disposal of the Victoria Park endowments, sufficient of these being linked with Hartley College to found three Chairs, these by their names recalling the old Ranmoor College and two greatly honoured laymen of the ex-United Methodist Church, whilst a goodly sum was also ear-marked for scholarships and bursaries at Hartley College. That College, in grateful recognition of this historic event and the generosity attending it, has been allowed by the Conference to adopt as its designation ' The Hartley Victoria Methodist College '. Still more recently there have been changes in the tutorial staff. The Rev. A. L. Humphries, after forty-eight years in the ministry, thirty-three of which had been spent in the service of the College, felt called upon to retire from the active ministry. So also did Professor Hirst, though he is continuing as a supernumerary to render part-time service as an Assistant Tutor. Mr. H. Crowther, LL.B., who was the Treasurer of the Victoria Park College, has been appointed co-Treasurer of Hartley Victoria with Mr. Gerrard, a similar arrangement applying also to the Secretaryship. So the life of the College has moved on, but amid all the changes which the years have brought Hartley College, whilst cherishing the memories and traditions of its past, is, under its new name and conditions, as eager as ever to serve the cause of evangelical truth and to promote the well being of Methodism.

CHAPTER XII
VICTORIA PARK AND RANMOOR COLLEGES
By
G. G. HORNBY, M.A., B.D.

I

FREE METHODIST COLLEGE

On the western border of the residential area known as Victoria Park, Manchester, is a building which used to bear this inscription cut in stone. It consisted originally of three dwelling-houses, which were purchased by the United Methodist Free Churches and adapted to serve the purposes of a Theological Institution. The total cost was about £3,000. This was not, however, the beginning of special ministerial training in this Church. The Annual Assembly of 1871 put an end to a discussion that had lasted for some years by setting apart as theological tutor the Rev. Thomas Hacking, a steady promoter of ministerial culture, and empowering a committee to make the necessary provision. The debate in the Assembly furnishes interesting reading. The objections to a College were earnestly stated. The students would lose their piety and zeal ; they would become proud ; they would be standardized to the pattern of their tutor. An alternative suggestion was made that accepted candidates should live by twos and threes in the homes of senior ministers, and should in this way be prepared for their life-work. There was another proposal that the Connexional Editor should be the Theological Tutor—as if the latter office would not require the full services of a minister ! But by a large majority the Assembly adopted the bold course. A house in Stockport Road was rented and suitably furnished. The library of the late Rev. James Everett was purchased for £300 and placed there. And in 1872 Mr. Hacking and six students came into residence. The tutor was responsible for instruction in Biblical and theological subjects as well as for general oversight; and supplementary classes in English language and literature, Greek, Logic and Mental and Moral Philosophy were taken at Owens College (now the Manchester University). The students preached on the Sundays in the chapels of the denomination, and during the week they engaged in pastoral visitation in the neighbourhood under the guidance of ministers.

The Theological Institution soon outgrew its temporary home. The Assembly of 1876 decided to have larger and more convenient premises, and in the following year the transference was made. Seven senior students came from the house in Stockport Road. As one of them, the Rev. G. H. Hinchliffe, says : ' It was like going from the kitchen to the drawing-room. Though the latter was a very modest building, it was princely when compared with the former '. Nine freshmen were admitted, so that there were sixteen in all in a building that had accommodation for twenty men. The routine, as described by Mr. Hinchliffe, was on the lines that have been preserved in the main throughout the history of the College—classes in the morning, recreation or visitation in the afternoon, private study in the evening. There was a class-meeting on the Friday night at which the men spoke of their religious experience. Later this became a students' prayer-meeting. Mr. Hacking was determined to prove that there was no foundation for the fears of some good people that College would spoil the men, and he devoted special attention to preparation for the pulpit. Every Friday morning two students read outlines of sermons, which were criticized by their fellows and by the tutor. Mr. Hinchliffe tells of one man who failed to bring an outline in his turn, and was instructed to furnish one on the following Friday from the text: 'I do remember my faults this day'.

Mr. Hacking retired from the principalship in 1880, and after a brief interval was succeeded in 1882 by the Rev. Anthony Holliday, who held the position until 1894. He was noted for preaching ability and administrative capacity, and in his relations with the students he 'was at once father, brother, friend, and teacher' (*New History of Methodism* I.547). It was due largely to the first two Principals that the United Methodist Free Churches forgot their doubts and fears, and came to be proud of their College.

In 1896 Mr. (afterwards Sir) James Duckworth became Treasurer. Three years earlier he had felt the need of a forward movement at the College, and had undertaken the task of carrying it through. By his generous gift of £3,000 a new wing was built, and the premises were made more comfortable for the residents and better adapted to the work of tuition. It was due also to his leadership and labours and liberality that the accumulated debt of nearly £4,000 was wiped out and a further sum of £20,000 was raised as an Endowment Fund to provide a steady income for the future. These services were commemorated by a tablet that was placed in the entrance hall. Mr. Duckworth built up a very large business from meagre foundations; he took a prominent part in the local government of Rochdale, and was a keen politician, being for some years a Member of Parliament (for Middleton 1897–1900, for Stockport 1906–10). But he always had time and strength for his Church, and his devotion was recognized by his election as President of the United Methodist Free Churches in 1894. He was the second (and last) layman to be so honoured. In the Conference Resolution that records his death he is termed the 'second founder' of the College. It was mainly by his effort and sacrifice that its finances were placed on a sound basis and that it was equipped for expanding service.

The first Principal to enjoy this larger opportunity was the Rev. Thomas Sherwood, a man of quiet, simple dignity, an honest and fearless thinker, well read in philosophy and theology. In his time the normal course for students was extended from two years to three, and a resident tutor was appointed to share the responsibility of the extended curriculum. The Rev. J. T. Brewis, B.A., B.D., who had already given part-time service for six years, entered in 1912 upon that intimate relation with the College which passed into the Principalship and has continued unbroken (save for the War period) up to the present.

This is a convenient place for referring to others who served as visiting tutors, supplementing the teaching of the theological tutor and the Owens College classes. In this capacity valuable help was given from time to time by various ministers: the Revs. J. Kirsop, J. Taylor, J. Twigg Taylor, W. Redfern, Ralph Abercrombie, M.A., A. Jones, and by two laymen of outstanding worth— R. J. Lloyd, M.A., D.Litt., and A. S. Peake, M.A., D.D.

The name of Dr. Peake will ever be associated with the Hartley College, and comes up most suitably in Chap. XI of this book. Dr. Lloyd, who taught mainly in Latin and Logic, was a man of remarkable personality. He was largely self-taught, but amassed a scholarship that won from the University of London the degree of Doctor of Literature. He was a keen philologist and delighted to pursue a word through half a dozen languages. He was associated with Dr. Murray in the earlier stages of the preparation of the *Oxford Dictionary*. He was a convinced Free Churchman and a loyal member of the United Methodist Free Churches. The resolution passed by the Annual Assembly after his death describes him as ' a man of great learning, modest and unassuming, deeply interested in the education of the students '.

2

RANMOOR COLLEGE

MINISTERIAL training in the Methodist New Connexion began in 1835 when one of its leading ministers, Thomas Allin, received some accepted candidates into his family and supervised their studies. The same service was rendered later by the Revs. William Cooke and James Stacey. In 1857 the Conference resolved that a Theological Institution should be established, and that it should be in the neighbourhood of Manchester. Nothing, however, was done until 1860. In that year Mr. Thomas Firth of Sheffield died. He was keenly interested in the training of the ministers of his Church, and in his will left £4,500 for the support of a Theological College on the conditions that it should be in the neighbourhood of Sheffield, and that it should be established within four years of his death. The Connexion responded to the challenge and raised £6,000 as a building fund. A suitable site was purchased at Ranmoor, a lovely suburb of Sheffield, and a College was erected with accommodation for sixteen students. It was opened in 1864 at a total cost of £8,700. The first Treasurer was Mr. Mark Firth, brother of Thomas and a generous donor to the College Funds, and when he retired from office in 1877 the debt on the building was wiped out. Mr. Thomas Firth's legacy became the nucleus of an endowment which ultimately reached the sum of £9,000.

At the start there were two tutors, the Revs. Samuel Hulme and James Stacey, the latter being Resident Tutor and Governor. This arrangement lasted for only twelve months : and on Mr. Hulme's retirement no successor was appointed through lack of funds. Mr. Stacey was responsible for all the tuition as well as for the government of the College. This heavy task he discharged admirably. Himself a native of Sheffield he was

eager that the College should stand well in the regard of
the citizens.   He was a versatile scholar with an acute
mind and a power of chaste expression.   A University
Professor who came into close connexion with him has
told me that he never met a finer mind than Dr. Stacey's.
The College was highly fortunate in its first Principal.

In 1876 Dr. Stacey, whose health had always been
frail, retired from the Principalship, though for three
years longer he served as Tutor.   The Rev. Dr. William
Cocker, a notable preacher and a favourite speaker on
the political platform, was Principal from 1876 to 1886.
He had as assistants, after Dr. Stacey, the Rev. B. B.
Turnock, M.A., a young man of great promise who died
prematurely after a few months, and the Rev. Dr. J. C.
Watts, who was then stationed in Sheffield.   After Dr.
Watts left (1883), it became the custom for the students
to go to Firth College (another example of the wise
generosity of the Firth family : it has grown to be the
Sheffield University) for training in classics.

Dr. Cocker was succeeded by the Rev. Dr. T. D.
Crothers (1886–1898).   He was a widely-read theologian
and a keen dialectician, who revelled in such works as
Butler's *Analogy of Religion*.   As his appointment drew to
a close there became manifest in the Connexion a movement for a change in College policy that would keep it in
line with the changing outlook in theological thought.
The three successive Principals had been worthy expon-
ents of traditional Methodism ; but it was felt by the
younger leaders of the Church that the time had come for
the training of the ministry to be in the hands of one who
possessed, in addition to a glowing Methodist experience,
a sympathetic knowledge of recent developments in
Biblical criticism and theology in general.   After a close
vote such an one was elected in the person of the Rev.
J. S. Clemens, B.A., a minister of twenty-two years'
standing.   The election was justified in the result.
Mr. Clemens proceeded to the degrees of B.D. and D.D.

(in St. Andrews University) ; and it is a sufficient tribute
to his scholarship that Dr. Hastings called upon him for
contributions to his *Dictionaries*.

The next step in the development of the new policy
was the appointment of the Rev. E. W. Hirst, M.A.,
B.Sc., as Tutor (1903).   It now became possible to extend
the period of tuition.   From the establishment of the
College a three years' training was intended ; but practical necessities had reduced it (except in rare instances)
to two years.   In 1910, however, the normal course was
extended to three years.

Something should be said about the activities of the
students outside the class-room.   Ranmoor was always
a small community ; and the spheres of service that are
open to a large college were outside its scope.   But there
were large demands on the students for pulpit work,
especially in the Sheffield Circuits, and in the days before
facilities of transport became accessible they were very
tired men that dragged themselves up the hill on Sunday
nights.   Some visitation was done at the Firth Alms-
houses,   and, when the Nether Green Church was
opened near to the College, the students were active in
visiting the neighbourhood and conducting meetings.
Men of the third year for a time served this Church as
student-pastors.   For physical recreation there was
inadequate provision on the premises.   Beautiful for
situation as the College was, stretching along the highest
of three terraces, and overlooking the Endcliffe Vale,
the grounds were too small for organized sport.   There
was a little cricket, sometimes in the field of a hospitable
club, and a little tennis on private lawns.   But the staple
recreation was in walking the magnificent moors around
Sheffield that make that place (in Ruskin's words) ' a fine
city to live out of '.

It was a happy life at College.   The Principals and
Tutors were kindly as well as capable ; the Principals'
wives, who acted as matrons, were motherly ; successive

secretaries and treasurers, whose names cannot here be recorded, gave themselves whole-heartedly to the task of making the best of comparatively small resources. The very smallness of the community encouraged intimate friendships among the men. Ranmoor was the smallest College in Methodism, but no one will deny that it turned out good ministers.

The Jubilee of Ranmoor College marked the closing of it as a Theological Institution. The Union of 1907 had placed two such institutions at the service of the United Methodist Church—the other being the Victoria Park College in Manchester. (The Bible Christian Church had no College for the specific training of its ministers. It was in the habit of sending some of its accepted candidates to the Shebbear College, a boarding-school for boys in North Devon, where they received a course of instruction adapted to their special needs.) It was obvious that there was a waste of money and energy in maintaining two small institutions. And in spite of strong local sentiments few could deny that Manchester offered through its University better facilities than Sheffield for advanced training. After long deliberation it was decided to retain both colleges for a time, but, when the opportunity came, to sell both buildings and erect a new College. Six years after the union (1913) Ranmoor became the home of the first-year students and Victoria Park of the second and third-year men. Dr. Clemens remained as Governor, and it was arranged that he and the Victoria Park staff should interchange tutorial service.

The new arrangement was not allowed time to justify itself. Before it had come to a second year the Great War broke out and Ranmoor was taken over as a hostel by the Teachers' Training College. The students enlisted, and Dr. Clemens entered Circuit work again. By the time the War was over the United Methodist Church had decided to bring all accepted Candidates for its ministry

to Victoria Park for their training. In 1919 Ranmoor
College was sold to the Sheffield Education Authority as a
centre for training instructors in physical culture. It is
now used as a nurses' hostel. The purchase money
(£11,628) with the endowments (£9,033) doubled the
endowment fund of Victoria Park. Some of the furniture and part of the library were also sent to Manchester.
The Hobill Library (a valuable collection of Methodist
literature) and the portraits of Principals and others were
housed for the time being in the School of the Nether
Green Church. They have now been transferred to the
Hartley Victoria College. And the honoured name
'Ranmoor' lives on in the designation of the Chair
of Church History and English at that College.

The story of many of what used to be called 'Dissenting Academies' is not unlike that of Ranmoor. They
have been erected and maintained by sacrificial gifts in
order to train an educated ministry ; they have struggled
to do this with small resources, and their success has been
far beyond what might have been expected. When
their work has been done, they have been merged in
larger and better-equipped institutions. The value of
their contribution to the religious life of England is
beyond computation. Those who founded and supported Ranmoor, those who taught and studied within
its walls, have good reason for joy and gratitude.

(This article has drawn much from an account of
Ranmoor College by the Rev. Henry Smith, which was
published in the *Methodist New Connexion Magazine* in
1901. Grateful acknowledgements to Mr. Smith are
here tendered.)

3

UNITED METHODIST COLLEGE

THE union of 1907 placed two theological Colleges at the service of the United Methodist Church. The smaller was Ranmoor College (Sheffield) which was founded in 1863 to train ministers for the Methodist New Connexion. At Victoria Park there was accommodation for twenty-two students ; at Ranmoor for sixteen. Neither was large enough by itself to meet the needs of the united Church. Neither could be readily enlarged. At Ranmoor, where there was adequate space, the cost would have been great ; at Manchester, which was much the better locality for a theological College, the site was too narrow. After long deliberation it was decided to retain both Colleges for a time but, when the opportunity came, to sell both buildings and erect a new College. Six years after the union (1913) Ranmoor became the home of the first-year students and Victoria Park of the second and third-year men. The Rev. David Brook, M.A., D.C.L., became Principal of both Colleges in this year ; the Rev. J. S. Clemens, B.A., D.D., who had been the Ranmoor Principal since 1898, remained there as Governor, and the Rev. J. T. Brewis, B.A., B.D., who had been tutor at Manchester since 1906, completed the staff.

The new arrangement was not allowed time to justify itself. Before it had come to a second year the Great War broke out. Both buildings passed into other hands for the time being. The tutors went into circuit work. Most of the students enlisted in the Army, and two of them laid down their lives. An oak tablet commemorating these two men was afterwards placed in the common-room at Victoria Park, where they had been students, and as a further memorial a sum of £100 was set aside, the interest of which was to supply books annually for native Chinese ministers. The fund for these purposes was raised by the students.

The Victoria Park College was reopened in 1919 under the principalship of Mr. Brewis. Now began the period of co-operation with Hartley Primitive Methodist College which was ultimately to result in a complete amalgamation. It came about in this way. At Victoria Park there were sixteen students, of three different years, and but one tutor. It was manifestly impossible for Mr. Brewis to undertake the whole of the tuition, and it was arranged that the students should go to Hartley daily and take its curriculum, and that Mr. Brewis should help the Hartley staff in the teaching. After the Victoria Park staff was enlarged in 1920 by the arrival of the Rev. E. W. Hirst, M.A., B.Sc. (tutor at Ranmoor 1903–13), and the Rev. G. G. Hornby, M.A., B.D., the co-operation was continued, greatly to the advantage of both Colleges. The tutors were able to specialize ; the language classes in each year were divided, so that the quicker students could move faster and the slower could make sure of what they learnt ; subjects that had been outside the range of one or other of the Colleges were brought on to the joint curriculum ; special classes for men aiming at a London University degree were established. The classes last mentioned were to the profit mainly of the United Methodist students for whom (unlike the Primitive Methodist students) there were no funds available to meet the cost of the five years' course necessary for a degree in divinity at the Manchester University. For the normal curriculum the commodious premises of the Hartley College were used, but a few special classes, including a sermon class, met at Victoria Park. The Victoria Park College, however, although little used for teaching purposes, was not a mere hostel. It carried on its proper traditions, inherited from previous generations of students ; it maintained its special activities, such as the annual effort for Foreign Missions. It had a life of its own, all the more intimate because of its fewer residents.

A few years later the Victoria Park College became too small to house the number of students required for the ministry of the United Methodist Church. As has been pointed out, no one ever thought it would be adequate to that purpose, and a new College had been in prospect from the time of union. But the negotiations for a wider Methodist Union had now begun ; and it was obviously a foolish policy to build a new Methodist College in a city where there were already two—Hartley and Didsbury Wesleyan Methodist College—both large and commodious and well equipped. For the time being it was decided to house at Hartley the students for whom there was no room at Victoria Park. There were now Primitive Methodists and United Methodists living under the same roof as well as sitting side by side at class.

For fifteen years the co-operation continued, and the comradeship both between tutors and between students grew ever closer. On the joint staff were eight tutors —reduced to seven in 1928 when one of the Hartley tutors, the Rev. Dr. W. Lansdell Wardle, took over the additional responsibility of the Governorship. There were generally well over a hundred students (once or twice about a hundred and thirty) under tuition. The scope of the curriculum was wide. In the three years' normal course it covered Hebrew and Greek ; Biblical Exegesis, Introduction and Theology ; Systematic Theology ; Logic, Psychology and Metaphysics ; Social and Moral Philosophy ; Christian and Comparative Ethics ; English ; Church History and Modern European History ; Homiletics and Pastoral Theology ; Elocution ; Training of Youth. The wisdom of the experiment in joint working was fully manifested.

4

THE COLLEGE AFTER UNION

AT the union of 1932 the Methodist Church found itself
in possession of three Colleges in Manchester, and at once
felt ' the embarrassment of riches '. The three came into
close fellowship, and there was some interchange of
tutors' services. But the many amalgamations of Circuits
resulted in a temporary superfluity of ministers and a
consequent reduction in the number of men in training
for the ministry. For these there was more than sufficient
accommodation in the seven Colleges of Methodism; and
it was clear that one College might be closed. Fortunately
for the peace of the newly established Church there was
no controversy over the question which that College
should be. The ex-United Methodists took the initiative
and were ready to sacrifice their personal inclinations and
affections in the interest of the whole Church. It was not
a small sacrifice, for the sentimental attachments that had
grown up through the long term of sixty years were
strong and precious. But the offering was made with a
cheerful spirit that was highly appreciated throughout
the Church.

Once the decision was taken events moved rapidly.
A scheme was prepared by the Victoria Park College
Committee and was accepted by the Ministerial Training
Committee in January 1934. The details of it were
worked out in sub-committees during the following
months, and a full report was presented to Conference
in July. Sanction was then given for the immediate
closing of the College and for the sale of the building.
But the action of the Conference had already been
anticipated up to this point—that a solemn service of
valediction was held in the College on June 11. The
Victoria Park College then ceased to exist. It had
served the United Methodist Free Churches for thirty-

VICTORIA PARK COLLEGE.

one years, the United Methodist Church for twenty-five years (twenty-two years if the interval of the War be allowed for), and the Methodist Church for two years.

But has it ceased to exist? Would it not be more correct to speak of a re-incarnation? As will be seen in the following statement, even the name lives on. Its traditions, its work, its spirit are transferred elsewhere; and every penny of the legacies bequeathed to it for theological training and of the endowments and other sums set apart for investment during its past history is still being used, and will continue to be used, for the purpose originally intended.

The co-operation of the last fifteen years with the Hartley College has become a complete union. Hartley is now Hartley Victoria—not an ideal name, but the best available. The students and staff have been transferred to Hartley Victoria College. The portraits of past Principals are on the walls of the new home. Most of the library is separately housed in an annexe; and a large part of the furniture has also been transferred.

Out of the Victoria Park and Ranmoor funds four chairs have been endowed at £10,000 each in harmony with the plan of the ex-Wesleyan Colleges. Three of the chairs are established at Hartley Victoria:

The DUCKWORTH Chair of New Testament Literature and Theology;

The LEWINS Chair of Philosophy;

The RANMOOR Chair of Church History and English.

The fourth—the VICTORIA Chair of Old Testament Language and Literature—is established at the Handsworth College. It will be noted that the titles of the chairs will keep in perpetual memory the names of the two Colleges now surrendered and of three treasurers of Victoria Park. The remainder of the General Funds (between seven and eight thousand pounds) is invested, and the interest is available for the ordinary purposes of the Ministerial Training Fund.

L

The moneys given by private benefaction for students at Victoria Park will be available for Hartley Victoria students for ten years, and will then be used as the Ministerial Training Committee determines. The capital value of these moneys amounts to nearly £9,000. Besides a number of prizes (mainly memorial) they include the ' Isaac and Ellen Aspin Scholarship ' of the annual value of £25, bequeathed by those whose name it bears ; the ' Miller Scholarship ' (the interest of a sum of £1,083 raised in 1890 as a memorial to the Rev. Marmaduke Miller) which entitles the holder to a fourth year at College (generally spent at the Manchester University); the sum of £2,000 given by the Misses Enid and Amy Jones (of Rochdale) in memory of Sir James Edward and Lady Jones, to found bursaries for students, and a bequest of about £3,750 under the will of the Rev. John Hammond in memory of himself and his brother, the Rev. Thomas Hammond. (The Hammond bequest amounted in all to £5,630, of which one-third was to be used for general purposes and two-thirds for the special benefit of students in bursaries and other ways.)

Some pain was unavoidable at the closing of a College which had a warm place in the hearts of United Methodists and was especially dear to those whose contact with it was most intimate—officers, tutors and students. Small as it was in comparison with the other Methodist Colleges and inconvenient in some respects, especially in the later years, it yet gave to hundreds of ministers not instruction alone but life-long friendships and inspiration. It was as dear to them as an ' alma mater ' is to her children. The closing ceremony on June 11, 1934, at which addresses were delivered by the last two ex-students to be called to the Presidential chair of the United Methodist Church, Revs. R. H. B. Shapland and William C. Jackson, M.A., was an experience that can never be forgotten. But the association with Hartley for fifteen years has eased the transference. And all at Hartley—com-

mittee, staff (both tutorial and domestic), and students—
have done everything in their power to make the new-
comers feel at home.   We are one—not in name only,
but in reality.

This is a history and not a prophecy.   One cannot look
far ahead ; but for the immediate future some provision
has already been made.   There are now five full-time
tutors at Hartley Victoria.   There is close co-operation
with the Didsbury College.   The mutual help given by
the two staffs since the union of the Churches will be
extended, and while each College will preserve its separate
corporate life every Tutor will be at the service of both
Colleges, and there will be continual fellowship both of
Tutors and of students for devotional and other purposes.
With two fine buildings, nine Tutors, an Assistant Tutor,
and accommodation for 160 students, Methodism in
Manchester has a unique opportunity for the training of
its ministers.   Exactly how these resources will be employed is not yet clear ; that they will be employed to
the full is assured.   Those who take the lead in ministerial training are giving most careful attention to this
problem ; in all concerned there is a keen sense of responsibility, coupled with the utmost good will and loyalty.
It is beyond question that the Manchester Colleges will
render invaluable service to Methodism and through
Methodism to the extension of the Kingdom of God ;
and to this the Victoria Park College, through its past
ministrations, its recent sacrifice of itself, and its renewed
life as a constituent part of Hartley Victoria, will make a
worthy contribution.

EPILOGUE

AFTER UNION

Now there are six Colleges; the five Colleges which before Union were Wesleyan, and Hartley Victoria, which tells of the coming together since Union of the two Colleges—Hartley and Victoria Park. The noble story of these two Colleges is told in this volume. There is close co-operation betwixt the Colleges of Hartley Victoria and Didsbury, and this has brought both together into a deepening fellowship. Owing to the greatly enlarged scope of the work of the Ministerial Training Committee, the Conference of 1933 appointed Rev. Thomas Naylor, B.A., as its first Secretary. We wish him every blessing in his new and most important task.

We look forward with confidence to the future of the Colleges, and believe that we shall be greatly inspired by our goodly heritage. We have been impressed by two things in reading our story of the past. The first is the heroic courage of our fathers, and their noble discontent, for each emprise called them to further effort. They worked in difficult days, and planned nobly—for they were men of vision and faith. Every extension of the work, then as now, called for new and larger responsibilities, to which they responded with gallant courage.

> God of our fathers, be the God
> Of their succeeding race.

They gave liberally, and prayed fervently, on behalf of the ministry of our Church. We believe that their children will be of the same spirit and temper—men of large-hearted generosity and faith—and that they will respond swiftly to the new calls made upon them. The days are difficult, large claims, both financial and spiritual, are made upon us. But in the spirit of sacrifice and prayer we will go forth to conquer. We have in the last few years successfully raised a large sum for capital expenditure ; but we still need a much enlarged annual income, and a wider and more democratic response to the appeal of the Ministerial Training Fund. The task of ministerial training must be not the hobby of a few, but the passion of all of us.

The second thing which has greatly impressed us is that our fathers never confused the means with the end. They sanctified the means in order to reach the goal, but they always clearly saw the end. They believed that there had been given to them the glorious privilege of winning the world for Christ, and that knowledge rightly used was a necessary ally in this divine crusade. They set out to equip students to be pastors and men of evangelical passion, and they kept rigorously to this aim. They called their fund which provided the sinews of war by a somewhat clumsy name—The Theological Institution Fund—but the name stood for something distinctly noble. They sought to give to men a deeper sense of God and divine things. Our new name for our work— The Ministerial Training—is much the best we could find. We got rid of the word ' Institution ' with its awkward associations. Although this new title has not a musical ring, it will suffice. For it testifies to the fact that our aim is the same as that of our fathers. The work of our Theological Colleges is the divine task of training men for the ministry of the Word and the Sacraments. Our work is near to life and to life's needs. Of Christian we read, ' He lifted up his eyes, and behold, there was a very stately palace before him, the name of which was Beautiful, *and it stood just by the highway* '. We pray that in each of our Colleges our talk, as was that in the House Beautiful, may be of divine things, and that all the teaching therein may make us more swift to hear, and more ready to respond to the divine command—' Go out into the highways and hedges, and constrain them to come in, that my house may be filled '.